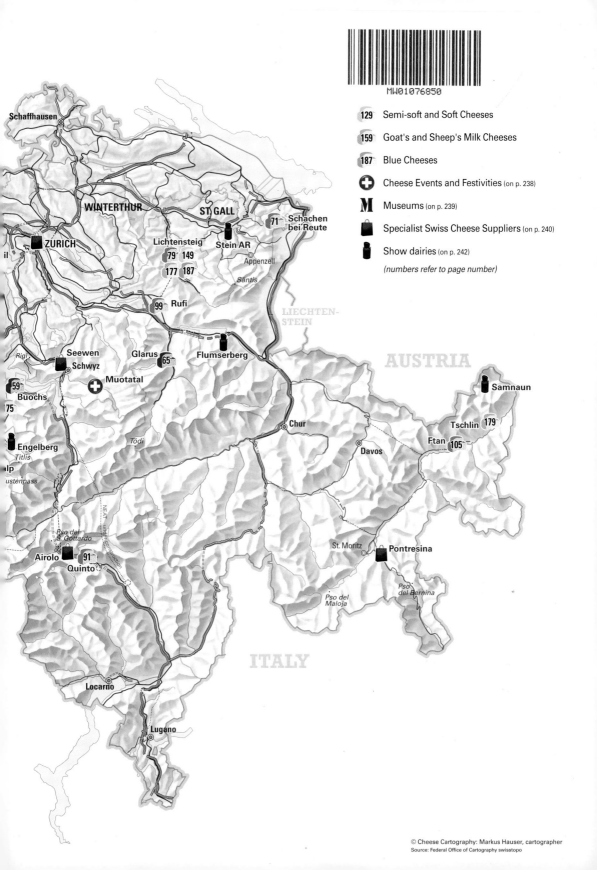

MW01076850

129 Semi-soft and Soft Cheeses

159 Goat's and Sheep's Milk Cheeses

187 Blue Cheeses

Cheese Events and Festivities (on p. 238)

M Museums (on p. 239)

Specialist Swiss Cheese Suppliers (on p. 240)

Show dairies (on p. 242)

(numbers refer to page number)

Schaffhausen

WINTERTHUR

ST GALL

71 Schachen bei Reute

ZURICH

Lichtensteig

Stein AR

79 149

Appenzell

177 187

Santis

99 Rufi

LIECHTEN-STEIN

Seewen

Schwyz

Glarus

Flumserberg

65

AUSTRIA

Muotatal

Samnaun

59

Tschlin 179

Buochs

Chur

Ftan 105

75

Tödi

Davos

Engelberg

Titlis

Ip

ustenpass

Pso del S. Gottardo

St. Moritz

Pontresina

Airolo

91

Quinto

Pso del Bernina

Pso del Maloja

ITALY

Locarno

Lugano

© Cheese Cartography: Markus Hauser, cartographer
Source: Federal Office of Cartography swisstopo

Cheese
slices of Swiss culture

by Sue Style
photographs by Nikos Kapelis

Bergli
books

Cheese
slices of Swiss culture

by Sue Style
photographs by Nikos Kapelis

Published with the support of
Switzerland Cheese Marketing AG
SO Appenzeller Käse GmbH
Interprofession du Gruyère AOC
Sbrinz Käse GmbH
EFBESA

Layout and design by:
eyeloveyou, Basel, www.eyeloveyou.ch
Resource and artwork editor: Ernst Roth
Art historian: Julia Hausammann

Historical artwork in this book is the property of the Roth Foundation (Roth Stiftung), Burgdorf, and is reproduced herein with their permission. Information about the art images in this book can be found on pages 246–249.

ISBN 978-3-905252-20-0

INTRODUCTION

Whether you're living in Switzerland, or an occasional visitor, or simply one who observes from afar, you can hardly fail to be aware of the country's deeply rooted cheese tradition. From the Ovaltine-coloured cows grazing in the meadows, the village dairies with milk churns lined up outside the back door, the alpine chalets with their copper vats warming over a wood fire, the autumn festivals with their stacks of cheese and flower-crowned cows, the well-furnished cheese counters in even the simplest supermarket – it's clear that cheese is at the heart of Swiss life. It's hardly surprising to learn what a prominent part it plays in the local diet: the Swiss consume almost 22 kilos of cheese per person per year, trailing only the Italians, French and Greeks in per capita consumption. There's hardly a meal, from breakfast to dinner, in which cheese does not play a part.

Over the centuries – certainly since Roman times, possibly even earlier – the Swiss have established a reputation as skilled cheese makers, especially for large, hard cheeses such as Gruyère and Emmentaler. Indeed most people – myself included – tend to think mainly in terms of these golden oldies when they think of Swiss cheeses. Few are aware of the seismic shifts that have been taking place in Switzerland's little cheese world of late. A key development was the demise in the 1990s of the Swiss Cheese Union, a government body which had held all cheese production, pricing and export in a vice-like grip since the first days of World War I. It's hard to overestimate the extent to which things changed once this restrictive body was wound up – one cheese maker describes the aftermath as *'après la libération'*, after the liberation.

So what's new? Well, as a matter of fact, quite a lot – as I discovered in the course of research for this book, travelling the length and breadth of this small country in summer, autumn and winter, rising at dawn to meet the cheese makers and watch them at work, marvelling at their passion and dedication – and sharing some memorable breakfasts along the way.

Firstly, Switzerland's grand old cheeses seem to have a new spring in their step. In the past ten years many of them have been elevated to AOC status (*Appellation d'Origine Contrôlée*, see page 244), giving long overdue protection of their names, restricting their area of production and strictly regulating all aspects of the cheese-making process. There's also renewed respect and recognition for alpine cheeses, and a determination to preserve this ancient model of cheese making based on the annual transhumance, the seasonal movement of farmers and their herds up into the alpine pastures in summer.

The second exciting development, also directly attributable to the collapse of the Swiss Cheese Union, is the extraordinary burst of creativity that's been released amongst a new generation of Swiss cheese artisans. Rather than making 'also-rans' in the familiar hard and semi-hard cheese mould, these gifted cheese makers are moving into spectacular, soft bloomy-rind cheeses and stinky, washed-rind varieties – not hitherto Switzerland's forte. Also new is the appearance of some fine goat's and sheep's milk cheeses. And finally, a few outstanding Swiss blue cheeses are making a cautious debut.

In Switzerland, small is beautiful – and nowhere more so than in the realms of cheese making, which remains reas-suringly small-scale. Partly, I believe, this is due to an instinctive, deep-seated Swiss mistrust of anything too big; and partly it's down to geography – 40 per cent of Swiss farms are in the Alps and Prealps, where there's simply no room for large holdings. Another reassuring fact – for those who like rich, complex, full-flavoured cheeses that taste of where they're made – is that raw (unpasteurised) milk is the norm. In Switzerland around 80 per cent of cheeses are made from raw

milk, compared with less than 20 per cent in France.

At a conservative estimate, Switzerland has at least 450 different kinds of cheese, a number which – I was assured by the people at Switzerland Cheese Marketing – is increasing steadily year on year. The hardest task in putting together this book was deciding which cheeses to include. To cover all 450 was clearly impossible; the challenge was to make a selection that would represent and encapsulate the work of Switzerland's skilled cheese artisans. Inevitably this is a personal selection, by no means an exhaustive one but, I hope, a representative one.

At cheese competitions the cheeses are typically classified according to hardness, ranging from the hardest to the softest. This is the system I've used in this book, which falls into five sections: hard and extra-hard varieties, semi-hard types, soft cheeses, those made from goat's and sheep's milk, and some blue cheeses. There are several examples of each kind, drawn from different parts of the country, each one forming a chapter of its own. Each chapter is a kind of vignette, depicting someone who makes this type of cheese, explaining why the cheese is made there, how it's done, what it tastes like and where to buy it.

Cheese makers are gifted artisans, in love with their product and delighted to introduce it to an appreciative audience. Many visitors to Switzerland are surprised to learn that it's often possible to visit these artisanal dairies – look out for the words *Käserei, Fromagerie, Laiterie, Sennerei* or *Lataria* and the telltale milk churns outside. Put your head around the door, show an interest and the chances are you'll be invited in to take a look. In some of the larger, more sophisticated ones you may be asked to don hairnet, shoe coverings and an overall to visit the premises. At alpine cheese dairies, which are often quite rudimentary and frequently only accessible on foot, stout hiking boots will be all that's required. And be prepared for an early start. The cows are milked at dawn and cheese making starts soon after, so dairy visits are definitely not for laggards or lie-abeds.

This book has been an extraordinary adventure, taking me and the photographer, Nikos Kapelis, on a journey into the farthest corners of this small, landlocked, mountainous country in search of Switzerland's finest, hand-crafted cheeses, both ancient and modern. Everywhere we travelled, we were received with unfailing courtesy, warmth, generosity – and with a certain degree of bemused curiosity.

Early-morning visits by British food writers and Greek photographers are probably not everyday occurrences in Swiss cheese dairies, yet these skilled, hard-working craftsmen and women coped calmly with our presence, manoeuvring their way deftly around us to do their work, halting the cheese-making process at strategic moments in order to be photographed and patiently answering our many questions. All of them are mentioned by name in the text. We salute them for their passion and dedication and we thank them for opening their dairies, chalets and homes to us.

As you set out on your own discovery of Swiss cheese, whether leafing through the pages of this book from the comfort of your armchair or on your own personal journey around the country with the book packed into your rucksack, I hope you'll have at least half as much enjoyment and enrichment as we have had along the way.

Sue Style, Bettlach, August 2011

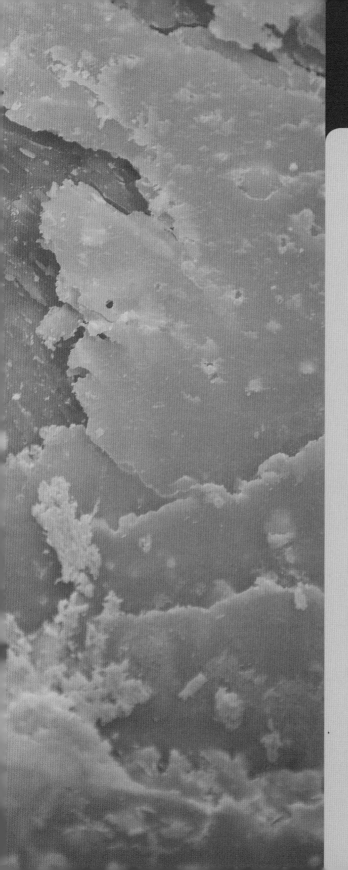

HARD AND EXTRA-HARD CHEESES

These are the grandfathers of the Swiss cheese family, with a history that goes back centuries. All were made originally in small alpine dairies, during the summer months only. For some – Gruyère d'alpage AOC, L'Etivaz AOC, Berner Alpkäse and Alp Sbrinz – this is still the case. In the nineteenth century, Swiss cheese making came down into the valleys for the first time, enabling hard cheeses such as Emmentaler, Gruyère and Sbrinz to be made in greater quantities and all year round.

The starting point for all of these is raw milk. Pasteurisation, which kills off all known microbes including the crucial flavour-conferring ones, is explicitly ruled out in the specifications laid down for these cheeses. During the cheese-making process, the milk is gently warmed, the curds are cut very small and then heated to a temperature well short of pasteurisation. Finally the cheeses are heavily pressed and salted. Each of these steps is designed to eliminate as much moisture as possible from the finished cheese, giving it extraordinary ageing qualities and allowing it to be matured without spoilage for anything from several months to some years.

Emmentaler AOC

For anyone embarking on a Swiss cheese exploration, the Emmental is a good place to start. As you wander through its gently undulating *Höger* and *Chräche* (hills and narrow valleys), past massive timbered farmhouses draped in great overhanging roofs and decked out in summer with a riot of geraniums, you'll find plentiful evidence of the region's rich dairying past. For hundreds of years, great wheels of Emmentaler cheese have rolled out of the village dairies of this famous valley.

Evidence of some kind of hard cheese being made in the area goes back to the thirteenth century, though for lack of precise descriptions, we can't know how it looked or tasted. What's certain is that it bore little resemblance to today's giant wheels, for early Emmentaler – in common with all of Switzerland's traditional hard cheeses – was made on a small scale in tiny mountain dairies and in the summer months only.

The summer grazing pastures or alps, sometimes owned by Bernese absentee landowners, sometimes owned directly by the farmers, were worked by cowhands known as *Küher*. These were drawn from the ranks of the non-inheriting sons of Emmentaler farming families. According to local law, the youngest son (not the eldest, and never the daughters) stood to inherit the farm, but to do this, he must compensate his siblings. At any given moment there were likely to be a number of skilled young chaps floating about the valley with money in their pocket, time on their hands and farming and cheese-making skills under their belt – but no land and no farmhouse. A logical step was to hire themselves out as *Küher*. In the eighteenth century, Emmentaler's golden age, many of these *Küher* became veritable cheese entrepreneurs, making and selling their cheeses both at home and abroad.

In the nineteenth century, the Emmental was the first region to bring its cheese making down from the mountains into the valleys. The village *Käserei* or cheese dairy was born. Freed from the constraints of the summer transhumance, Emmentaler could now be made all year round. This greatly simplified model of cheese making together with increased milk quantities meant that cheeses became steadily larger, a development that made perfect economic sense, since the duty on cheese for export was calculated on a per cheese basis rather than according to its weight.

An impressive beast, today's Emmentaler AOC measures about a metre across and around 20 cm high with an average weight of 100 kilos (over 200 lbs) – like a huge tractor tyre without the treads.

The Alps

An alp (written in lower case) is a summer pasture situated on steep slopes above the valley, where farmers take their animals for the annual transhumance. The Alps refers to the whole, great, snow-capped European mountain range that stretches from Austria and Slovenia in the east through Italy, Switzerland, Lichtenstein, Germany to France in the west.

Its flesh – sweetly yielding and mildly nutty – is a pale primrose-yellow. While Swiss production is not limited to the Emme Valley, it is here that the cheese was born and continues to be made – in small village dairies like the one I visited in Oberhünigen, southeast of Bern.

The dairy is jointly owned by the farmers who supply the milk; the Glauser family are tenants. Work starts at 5 a.m. for Christoph Glauser and his apprentice (who is learning, in today's parlance, to be a *Milchtechnologe* or milk technologist). The

Urs Glauser with his Emmentaler AOC.

floors are scrubbed and sluiced with high pressure hoses, sundry items of cheese-making equipment are readied – churns, plastic scoops and pails, cheese harps and stainless steel paddles for breaking and stirring the curds.

Soon the milk starts to arrive from the neighbouring farms. The average holding is around 15 cows, explains Christoph, mainly Simmentalers and red Holsteins. "And they all have names – when you only have 15 cows, they're all pretty special," he adds with a grin.

The milk is weighed, checked and pooled with last night's delivery in a

giant vat. From its 6,500-litre contents will come five mighty wheels of cheese – and an awful lot of whey. Two different kinds of starter bacteria are added, one to acidify the milk, the other to ensure formation of the all-important holes, as well as a dose of rennet to coagulate the milk.

We leave the starter bacteria and rennet to get on with their work and adjourn to the kitchen above the dairy for a breakfast of milky coffee, well-crusted country bread, freshly patted butter, slivers of young Emmentaler and Frau Glauser's home-made apricot jam.

Back in the dairy, once the curds are firmly set, Christoph activates the cheese harps which cut the curd into rice-sized grains. Emmentaler is a 'cooked' cheese, explains Christoph, meaning that the curds are now heated so that as much whey as possible will be released, giving a cheese with low moisture and firm, dense texture, which will allow the cheese to be matured to a ripe old age. Subsequent steps in the process – pressing, salting, ageing – will all contribute to this objective.

The cheese harp starts to cut the curd.

Finally curds and whey are pumped over into tall, drum-like plastic moulds, whey cascading out of the bottom and sides and into a trough. As the whey drains off, the upper part of the mould is lifted away, leaving a lower 'corset' which now braces and shapes the newborn cheese.

Numerals for today's date and the Glausers' identification code (both made of casein, an edible milk by-product) are laid on top and the whole thing is crowned with the distinctive red and white Emmentaler AOC label, which completely covers the upper surface and will fuse with the rind. The cheeses will be pressed overnight, to go down later into their salt bath, and thence into a cool cellar where they will rest for a few days to firm up. The final step is a 6 to 8-week spell in a warm, moist room where the famous holes will form.

Aah, the holes! They're an essential part of the Emmentaler story, stresses Christoph. The AOC rules actually stipulate the extent and size of them: there should be at least 1000 and no more than 2000 per cheese, each with a diameter of between 1 and 4 cm (though it's not clear who's counting – or measuring – them). The specific Emmentaler culture added at the beginning contains a particular bacteria (otherwise known as 'the hole-maker'), which gobbles up and converts the cheese's lactic acid to produce carbon dioxide bubbles, which are the holes. At the end of my visit, Christoph took me down to the cellar to see this in action. The upper surface of the young cheeses, which had started out perfectly flat, had begun to swell up and the sides to bulge out. Clearly those hole-making bacteria were hard at work.

Carrying chunks of cheese like this keeps Urs Glauser fit.

Emmentaler AOC

Starting in the 1870s, the Swiss made successive attempts to protect the name of their big cheese with holes, but were thwarted at every turn, notably by the Germans and the French who claimed the right to make their own 'Emmentaler' or 'Emmental'. In 2006 the Swiss succeeded in securing an *Appellation d'Origine Contrôlée* (AOC, see page 244) for Swiss-produced Emmentaler. This protected status regulates how the cheese is made in Switzerland and confines production to a handful of cantons. To be sure you're getting the real thing, look for the label of Emmentaler Switzerland.

What about taste? There's a perception – strenuously countered by Christoph – that the big cheese with the big holes has little flavour. A lot depends on age – and serving temperature too. Emmentaler should never be served too cold. "Take it out of the fridge at least a couple of hours before you eat it," counsels Christoph.

Young Emmentaler – between four and eight months old – is by nature demure and mild-mannered. For me, it's reminiscent of one of those paintings by the Bernese artist Albert Anker, all embroidered smocks, apple-cheeked girls, breakfast tables laid with buttered *Züpfe* (the classic Bernese braided bread) and warm milk. The flesh is fragrant, firm but supple, the flavour mildly nutty with a good balance of sweetness and acidity.

Aged over eight months, the cheese starts to flex its muscles a bit and it begins to lose its gentle, amenable character. The strongest (labelled *Höhlengereift* or cave-ripened) is matured for at least 12 months, of which a minimum of six must be in special limestone caves. After this time it develops a dark brown crust and the flavour is intensified. If you've always reproached Emmentaler for its lack of character, this may be the one to change your mind.

Urs Glauser extracts a plug of cheese to test.

Käserei Oberhünigen
3504 Oberhünigen BE

Tel. 031 791 02 58
glauser.urs@bluewin.ch
www.silofrei.ch/hersteller/
portraits/glauser

Le Gruyère Switzerland AOC

Gruyère AOC is the grandee among Swiss cheeses. Like Emmentaler AOC – which it has recently overtaken in production terms – it has been much copied but seldom matched. It has more flavour than Emmentaler – and few or no holes. Between them, these two account for almost 30 per cent of all cheese produced in Switzerland.

A large, hard, cooked cheese of the Gruyère type has been made in the mountainous regions of canton Fribourg in western Switzerland for centuries, certainly since the late Middle Ages. In its original homeland it was known simply as *caseus* or *fromage* ('cheese') to distinguish it from the soft, uncooked skim milk cheeses (*séré* or *sérac*) that were also commonly made. From its beginnings as a small-scale, locally consumed and traded mountain cheese, it gathered strength until by the eighteenth century it was the

principal source of income for the canton of Fribourg. Once the cheese began to be exported – Lyon was an important market – it needed a name, hence *fromage de gruiere* [sic]. Later this was shortened (and the spelling standardised) to gruyère.

The biggest change came about in the nineteenth century, when dairying began to nudge out cereal farming in the lowlands and cheese making came down from the mountains for the first time. Gruyère, formerly made only during the summer months in small alpine chalets, could now be made in village dairies all year round. This is the case for most Gruyère AOC nowadays. Alpine cheese made in the high summer pastures, once the norm, has become a niche product and makes up only a tiny part of the total Gruyère AOC picture (see Gruyère d'alpage AOC, page 29).

To get to grips with Gruyère AOC, I joined René Kolly, former head of Gruyère AOC's professional body, latterly President of Fromarte, the umbrella organisation for Switzerland's artisan cheese makers. Monsieur Kolly's official duties keep him busy, so increasingly his son Benoît makes the cheese at the family-owned Laiterie Le Mouret just south of Fribourg. "He's the one to get up at 5 a.m. now!" grins Kolly Senior. This pattern of sons (and occasionally daughters) following their fathers into small dairying businesses was to become a familiar one throughout my travels. I'd feared that Switzerland's cheese makers might be a dying breed with few likely successors. The reality was reassuringly different.

Benoît's first task of the day is to fetch the milk from the 35 farms in the neighbourhood that supply the dairy. A few

The different meanings of 'Gruyère'

To the dismay of the Swiss, ownership of the name Gruyère has long been contested and a cheese calling itself by that name is widely made outside Switzerland. A long overdue solution – something of a compromise – was found in 2001 when Swiss-made Gruyère obtained its *Appellation d'Origine Contrôlée*. To distinguish it from non-Swiss wannabes, the cheese's name is prefaced with the definite article: <u>Le</u> Gruyère AOC. Note too that <u>La</u> Gruyère is the region in canton Fribourg where the cheese originated, while Gruyères is the beautifully preserved, traffic-free castle-village once the seat of power of the Counts of Gruyère.

p. 22/23 →
The beautiful village
of Gruyère

SWITZERLAND

Suisse

Chemins de fer électriques de la
GRUYERE

farmers, who have only a handful of cows and live within walking distance of the dairy, wheel in their couple of churns on small barrows.

Lowland Gruyère dairies look very different from their alpine counterparts – larger, often purpose built and fully automated. But the basic programme is the same. First the morning milk joins the evening milk in the vat and is lightly skimmed. In goes the starter culture, which will acidify the milk, and at a decent interval the rennet is added to coagulate it. The milk is left quietly in the vat until the whole thing starts to resemble trembling blancmange. Next the curds are cut and stirred for about 30 minutes till the correct, rice-like granules form, then the mass is heated.

Finally the curds and whey are pumped over to a line of perforated plastic moulds and the whey drains off.

The cheeses are pressed overnight, and emerge next morning looking like beautiful white wedding cakes. After 24 hours' immersion in brine, the cheeses are moved down to the cellar to start their slow maturing. Every one of the cheeses (the Le Mouret dairy makes around 30 wheels every day, each weighing approximately 35 kilos) must now be turned and brushed daily with a salty solution. Salt fulfils numerous functions besides the obvious one of seasoning the cheese. It slows down the development of the starter bacteria, thus modifying the rate at which the cheese will ripen, as well as drawing out moisture from the rind and acting as a preservative.

Last year, admits Benoît with pride and evident relief, they invested in a robot that brushes and turns the cheeses – no more clambering up ladders, heaving out heavy cheeses by hand, turning, brushing and replacing them on the shelf. "The

only trouble is, now I have to go to the gym for my *musculation*!" (body-building), he grins.

The finished wheels are stacked to the roof in a huge, new, purpose-built, air-conditioned store room where they will remain for at least four months. It's an impressive sight. Each month Benoît checks on a batch that's nearing its four-month birthday. He shows me how he brings the cheeses down from the shelf and taps the

The curd is set, ready for cutting by the harp.

The curds and whey are pumped over to a line of perforated metal moulds and the whey drains off.

← Le Gruyère AOC stamp affixed to the top of the freshly moulded cheese.

Benoît Kolly at his daily cheese-brushing task.

crust enquiringly with a small, hammer-like instrument. The sound it makes gives a clue to the presence of holes and/or defects. Then he extracts a plug of cheese, examines it, sniffs it, pulls off a tiny piece to taste, and carefully replaces the plug.

Benoit's job is to judge when the cheeses are ready to move on to the specialist *affineurs* or cheese merchants who will complete the maturing. Five months is the minimum age at which Gruyère AOC may be sold. The official classification is 5–9 months for *classic* and from 10 months for *réserve*. You can buy Le Gruyère AOC direct from the dairy's shop which adjoins the dairy. They also have an exclusive

contract to supply Gruyère AOC to Globus, the upmarket Swiss department store with a renowned delicatessen.

What does Benoît look for in a fine Swiss cheese, I wondered. First of all, he says, if you cut a finger-sized piece and bend it, it should form a nice supple rainbow before it breaks; the flesh should be smooth and fine, melting on the tongue. The taste should be mouth-filling, with the telltale '*goût de noisette*' (nutty/hazelnut flavour) typically associated with this cheese. "And Gruyère AOC from Switzerland has hardly any holes," he grins in conclusion.

Benoît Kolly
Laiterie-Fromagerie du Mouret
Route de La Gruyère 6
1724 Ferpicloz FR

Tel. 026 413 11 07
bekolly@bluewin.ch
www.laiterie-du-mouret.ch

Le Gruyère d'alpage AOC

To get a feel for Gruyère as it was made in the old days, it's worth paying a visit to the Musée Gruérien in Bulle. The museum houses a rich collection of works of art and artefacts relating to farming and cheese making in the region, including some superb *poyas*, the stylised, naïf paintings which were formerly affixed to farmhouses throughout the canton. These celebrated paintings depict processions of people and cows as they make their way up to the high pastures for the summer transhumance.

One of them, painted by Sylvestre Pidoux in around 1840, is especially famous, thanks in part to its reproduction as a much-loved postcard. Look closely and you'll see that the horse-drawn cart at the head of the procession, driven by a smartly top-hatted *maître-armailli* (master cheese maker), is laden with all the cheese-making equipment necessary for making Gruyère on the alp – milking stools, an inverted, smoke-blackened copper vat, cheese cloths and wooden moulds and a wooden contraption like an inverted wheelbarrow (*l'oiseau*, the bird), which was used for carrying cheeses down to the valley.

One hundred and fifty years on, top hats have disappeared and trucks have supplanted horse-drawn carts. But almost everything else about the seasonal transhumance to the alpine pastures is unchanged. What is different is that in Pidoux's day, Gruyère d'alpage was the only kind of Gruyère that existed. Nowadays, the bulk of Gruyère AOC Switzerland – around 30,000 tonnes annually – is produced in lowland village dairies all year round. Gruyère d'alpage AOC (of which only around 480 tonnes are made) has moved from the norm to the niche.

A splendidly attired eighteenth-century Fribourg alpine herdsman.

A cheese merchant in a Fribourg market – note l'oiseau, the wooden contraption used for carrying cheeses to market.

Early one July morning I set off in search of some Gruyère d'alpage AOC, in the company of Renaud Burnier, a Mont Vully wine-grower who took me under his wing and promised to introduce me to a special alpine cheese maker. Somewhere between Bulle and Château d'Oex and just short of the village of Albeuve, we took a right turn up a dizzyingly steep, single-track road with passing places. Framing the beautiful, broad, sunlit prealpine valley was a range of jagged peaks. Below their creased and crinkled summits, still streaked with traces of snow, swathes of deep green spruces gave way in turn to subalpine pastures, intensely green now after the snowmelt and gaily splashed with dandelions, marguerites and pink and white clovers.

We slid to a halt below the tree line in front of a simple concrete and wood chalet marked with the name of the alp and its altitude: Théraulaz d'en Bas – 1295 metres. Some pink pigs – the chubby beneficiaries of whey from cheese making – basked contentedly in the early morning sunshine. A few curious Holstein calves, both red-and-white and black-and-white, peeped around a wall.

Whey and its numerous uses

When milk is coagulated by the addition of rennet, it separates into curds (which turn into cheese) and whey. Broadly speaking, for every kilo of cheese produced, there are ten kilos/ litres of whey. Disposal of whey can become a problem, particularly in an industrial setting. In Switzerland, where cheese making is generally small-scale, the problem is less acute. Most dairy farms and some cheese makers keep pigs which (in common with the calves) are fattened on whey. Its high nutritional value makes it appreciated by athletes and bodybuilders. Whey is also used to make the famous carbonated Swiss drink Rivella®. It comes in four different colours: red (the original drink, created in the 1950s to mop up all that whey, blue (a low-calorie version), green (flavoured with green tea), and a yellow one (based on soy rather than dairy milk extracts). Other creative uses for this by-product include cosmetic creams and sunscreens, whey baths and health cures.

We climbed the steps to the chalet to meet our cheese maker host for the morning, Jean-Louis Roch. Ruddy-faced, wreathed in smiles and sporting a single earring, he offered each of us in turn a dripping forearm to be shaken. According to my winegrower-guide, Jean-Louis had swept the board in the most recent Swiss Cheese Awards, winning not only best in class for his Gruyère d'alpage AOC, but also earning the title of Swiss Champion Cheesemaker. We were in good hands.

This was my first visit to an alpine dairy and impressions were vivid and memorable. In the middle of the room, which was not much bigger than an average-sized kitchen, a copper vat, blackened with wood smoke on the outside and gleaming within – just as Pidoux had painted it – was suspended over a crackling wood fire. It contained last evening's milk, left to stand overnight in large, shallow pans and relieved of some of its cream, together with the morning milk fresh from the cows in the milking parlour below the chalet. To these had been added some starter culture reserved from yesterday's cheese making, and a dose of rennet.

At the start of the season when milk yields are highest, explained Jean-Louis, he makes two or three cheeses per day, each weighing around 25 kilos. Alpine cheeses are smaller than lowland cheeses,

Decorated cowbells worn by the cows for the ascent to the alp in June and the descent in September.

which typically average 35 kilos. This is partly a hangover from the days when they had to be carried down from the alp on someone's back, and partly a reflection of the fact that work in a small alpine dairy is still almost entirely manual. As the season draws to a close and milk yields diminish, the rhythm is more like two cheeses one day and only one the next.

While the milk was warming, we were invited into the wood-panelled kitchen next door for steaming cups of coffee smoothed and enriched with gobs of cream from a small wooden tub (*dyètsè*) set in the centre of the table. Jean-Louis' son Sébastien joined us. He's apprenticed to a farmer in Solothurn, a German-speaking canton further north. "That way I can learn Swiss-German," he explains, adding "and I get to see how other people farm." Cheese making he's learning from his father, at weekends and during the holidays. Will Sébastien continue this great alpine tradition when his father retires, I wondered. "Definitely!" he responds vigorously. "*On doît absolument le maintenir*," chimes in his father ("we should certainly

Red-and-white and black-and-white Holsteins grazing the alpine pastures.

The copper vat is ready to be swung over the wood fire.

A typical wooden dyètsè filled with thick cream.

The milk is heated to the required temperature in the vat.

keep up this tradition"), adding that they get good support from the Fribourg national councillor, who is himself a farmer.

Back in the dairy, it was clear from the smoothly solidifying mass in the vat that the starter and the rennet had already set the milk off on its cheesy journey. Jean-Louis pressed the button to activate the cheese harps set into the mechanical arm straddling the vat. Once the granules were cut by the harps to the correct size – like grains of rice – he exchanged the harps for paddles and swung the vat across to the fire which he now stoked up to a fearsome heat.

At regular intervals Jean-Louis dipped a thermometer into the vat to check the temperature. Occasionally he would reach in and scoop out a handful of curds, squeezing the grains questioningly into a ball, then opening up his fist to check for the right texture, consistency and 'grip' (the grains must hold together firmly).

Once Jean-Louis judged the curds to his liking, he motioned to Sébastien and together they took hold of the four corners of a large, square, linen cheesecloth, leant into the vat and scooped up a load. They gathered up the corners of the cloth into a balloon-like bag, hoisted it high, gave the bag a squeeze and transferred it, steaming and dripping whey, to a circular cheese mould set before the window on the other side of the dairy.

Finally Jean-Louis leaned heavily on the curds to make sure they were well ensconced and patted a few stray grains firmly in place. The cheeses were dated (born, as it happened, on the Fourth of July), numbered (the 30th wheel this summer) and affixed with the identification plaque bearing Jean-Louis' number (CH-6062). Then he brought the four corners of the cheesecloth up over the top and tied them in a rough topknot.

The cheese harp is set in place.

Jean-Louis and helper lift the cheesecloth full of curds.

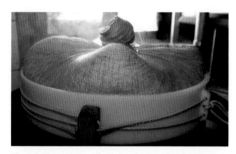

The cloth-wrapped curds are braced by the cheese mould.

Jean-Louis Roch brushes the new cheeses with salt.

For a hiking trail with a difference, try the Chemin du Gruyère, the Swiss Chocolate and Cheese Trail which starts in Charmey, takes in the Maison Cailler visitors' centre in Broc for a chocolate sampling and finishes with a taste of cheese in La Maison du Gruyère. See also the boxed text on page 46 about another part of this trail.

For more information go to: *www.myswitzerland.com/en/interests/hiking1.html*

Chemin du Gruyère

A well-aged hunk of Gruyère d'alpage AOC – without holes!

The cheeses would be pressed overnight and then put in a salt bath for a further 24 hours. For the first three weeks of their life, the wheels would be brushed with salt solution and turned regularly by Jean-Louis or Sébastien. Finally, most of the cheeses would go down to the valley to the cooperative in Charmey where their maturing would be completed. Jean-Louis has the right to keep some cheese for his own consumption and for private sale.

All Gruyère AOC, whether lowland or d'alpage, is aged for at least five months, though it would be akin to infanticide to eat such a fine cheese so young. Before we left, Jean-Louis selected an 18-month-old, 50 cm-diameter wheel from the wooden shelf in the cool cellar below the chalet and carved off a generous hunk for our inspection. The smooth, buttercup-yellow flesh was almost devoid of holes (Gruyère AOC Switzerland, unlike many foreign wannabes, has few or none), the rind was a rich, orangey-brown. He wrapped the piece carefully in waxed paper emblazoned with the proud Gruyère d'alpage AOC label.

Back home we cut slivers of the cheese, sniffed, nibbled and rolled it experimentally around our mouths. Faint suggestions of alpine flora, sweet mountain air and fugitive aromas of wood smoke preceded a powerful hit on the palate from the beautifully mature cheese, punctuated with tiny crunchy protein crystals.

Jean-Louis Roch with a freshly pressed cheese – 26 8 gives the date (26 August) and
the number 30 identifies this as the 30th wheel of the season.

Jean-Louis Roch
La Théraulaz d'Avau
in summer: in Albeuve
in winter: Chemin du Pouty 1
1689 Le Châtelard-près-Romont FR

Tel. 026 652 46 44

L'Etivaz AOC

L'Etivaz is an alpine cheese with attitude. Made in the Prealps of canton Vaud, for centuries it was subsumed anonymously into the Gruyère appellation. But with the dawn of the twentieth century, the makers of L'Etivaz had a vision: they would cut themselves loose from Gruyère and go it alone under their own name.

Their first smart move, in 1932, was to form a cooperative and build a cellar in the village of L'Etivaz, where cheeses from the various alps around the village would be gathered together and matured under optimal conditions. In 1945, L'Etivaz bravely stepped out of the Swiss Cheese Union, leaving it bereft of the safety net of subsidies but free to carve its own path. In 2000 L'Etivaz became the first cheese in Switzerland to protect its name by an *Appellation d'Origine Contrôlée* (AOC – see page 244). It now ranks among Switzerland's finest alpine cheeses, widely

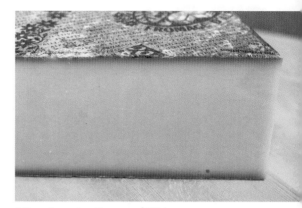

A fine piece of well-matured L'Etivaz.

available in good supermarkets and cheese stores, and greatly appreciated abroad, especially in France, its most enthusiastic and faithful export market.

Unlike Gruyère AOC, which is made in both lowland and alpine versions and throughout western, mainly French-speaking Switzerland, L'Etivaz AOC is exclusively an alpine cheese, made between 10 May and 10 October in mountainous areas of canton Vaud at altitudes of between 1000 and 2000 metres. A little smaller than Gruyère (around 22 kilos compared to Gruyère's 35), its rind is decorated with a delightfully distinctive *Scherenschnitt* label showing a couple of cut-out cows, a cheese maker bent low over his vat and a large wheel of cheese.

"We have over 70 producers scattered around our various alps," explains Christophe Magne, head of the L'Etivaz cooperative, "and their cheeses are all different – this is an artisan product." How does Magne account for these variations? Several factors contribute to the character

Paper cuts in Swizerland

Scherenschnitte (literally `scissor cuts`) are paper cuts or silhouettes which are popular decorative elements in Switzerland. In the seventeenth century, nuns in cloisters in various regions of Switzerland were making paper cuts with scissors or scalpels. Often these filigree images depict the traditional life of farmers and cheese makers in mountainous areas. Today, Swiss Scherenschnitt artists are enjoying new popularity and working with new themes. The one on the following pages is by Christian Schwyzgebel and made in Saanenland.

p. 38/39 →
A perfectly symmetrical Scherenschnitt or paper cut showing the cows processing up to the alp, cheese making top left and right, cheese finishing bottom left and right and the chalet lower centre.

of alpine cheese, he explains, including the time of year (milk's composition and quality changes during the course of the summer) and the altitude at which the chalet lies (the quantity and quality of the alpine flora grazed by the cows varies over the months, and between lower and upper pastures). Perhaps the most significant element is what Magne calls *'la main du fromager'* (the cheese maker's hand).

I went in search of a cheese maker's hand and found Claude-Alain Mottier. He and his wife Isabelle decamp from their valley farm up to the family alp every year from mid-June to mid-September. They're accompanied by their three children, their Polish helper Krzysztof, the family cat, and 45 cows.

"If you want to see the whole thing, you'll have to be up here by 6 a.m." warned Claude-Alain by mobile phone from the chalet. Clearly I'd need to spend the night close by. He mentioned a small inn in the village, then, somewhat hesitantly, ventured: "you could stay with us in the chalet, in the kids' *dortoir* (dormitory). It's pretty simple, but you're welcome to it." A plan was hatched to meet up with Isabelle as she came off duty at the local pharmacy

The (nervous) author, plus sundry baggage, ready for the ascent in the télépherique.

where she works part time. We would drive up the valley and park at the *téléphérique*, which would whisk us aloft to Les Arpilles, the alp at 1768 metres.

The *téléphérique* turned out to be a rudimentary iron cage with a couple of wooden benches nailed to the floor, the whole contraption suspended from a stout (we hoped) wire which disappeared up into the heights. We bundled in bags of clean laundry, boxes of potatoes, courgettes and salad from the Mottiers' vegetable garden down in the valley plus sundry cameras, tripods, sleeping bags and rucksacks.

Isabelle cranked up the phone that's wired to the chalet above, and instructed Claude-Alain and Krzysztof to switch on the generator for the power to haul us up. Then she pressed the button and jumped

The view on the way up.

A wistful young woman prepares her farewells before the cowherd sets off with the cows for the summer – though modern-day alpine cheese makers are often accompanied by family, in former times they spent the summer alone up on the alp.

A joyful reunion as the cowherd returns to the farm in the valley at summer's end.

Wooden dyètsès filled with cream skimmed off the milk before cheese making. Notice the handy way to keep the cream cool without a refrigerator. The opening in the thick stone wall creates a draft that cools the cream.

in after us. There was a brief lurch and we soared skywards.

Our parked cars soon paled to mere smudges way below. Anxieties about vertigo, safety, or dropping things over the edge of our little airborne cage were swept aside by breathtaking views of the jagged peaks of the Pays d'Enhaut ('the country up high'), now etched against the setting sun.

The Mottiers have three chalets on two different alps, each at a different altitude. They move around from one to another during the season depending on the state of the grass. "*Ici*" explained Isabelle as we swung to a halt just below the stone and wood chalet, "*on est au deuxième étage*" ("here we're on the second floor").

Soon we were feasting on freshly boiled potatoes and ham rolls bathed in a creamy, sunset-coloured sauce streaked with tomato purée and baked in the oven. Anticipating an early rise we headed to bed in good time. (I drew the long straw, dodged the *dortoir* and got the double bed in the kitchen.) Lulled by a gentle chorus of bells from the animals grazing all night outside the chalet windows I slept soundly, and woke soon after six.

Claude-Alain and Isabelle's day was already well under way. From the shallow pans of last night's milk set out on a long wooden sill in the cool room next to the dairy, Isabelle had skimmed a thick

Claude-Alain checks the curd to see if it is set...

...and begins to cut the curd in small pieces with the harp.

Isabelle and Claude-Alain lift the curds out of the vat.

The cheesecloth full of curds is lifted into the mould...

...the curds are settled in firmly...

layer of cream. This she poured into the typical decorated wooden tub, which she placed with its carved wooden spoon in the centre of the breakfast table. Cheese-cloths were rinsed, the newly kindled fire crackled and fussed. Next door Claude-Alain and Krzysztof forked fresh straw into the stall, ready for the cows. Time for breakfast.

Fortified with slabs of thickly crusted country bread, hand-patted butter, plum jam and luscious gobs of cream, spooned from their decorated wooden *dyètsè*, we set off to fetch the cows, fanning out on the steep hillside above the chalet, join-ing the chorus of whoops and shouts and rounding up the laggards. The cows made their unhurried way down to the cowshed adjoining the chalet, then stood patiently in line waiting to go indoors to be milked.

Cheese making could now begin. The evening milk (stripped of much of its cream, which had enriched our supper dish and the breakfast table) was tipped into the vat. This was topped up, bucket by bucket, with the fresh milk from the cows next door.

Then it was the usual pattern: first the starter culture kept back from yesterday's cheese making to acidify the milk, and rennet to thicken it. Once set, the curds were cut and the mass heated. Claude-Alain and Isabelle stationed themselves one on each side of the vat, dipped in the cheesecloth and scooped up the curds *à deux*. "What happens if you don't have a wife to help on the alp?" I asked. "*On ne fait pas de fromage!*" ("You don't make cheese") grinned Claude-Alain.

Once the cheeses had been formed, pressed, dated and numbered, they would get a preliminary brushing with salt solu-tion. Then they would be stored briefly in a cool room below the chalet, ready to go down to the cooperative within the next couple of days.

Here, resumed director Christophe Magne, they would be placed in a salt bath

Mature cheeses in L'Etivaz cellars down in the valley.

Detailed records are kept daily.

..weights are placed on top of the two cheeses...

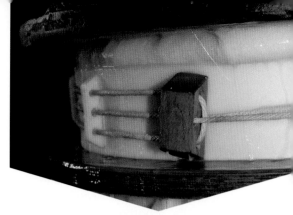

...the cords are tightened and the cheeses left overnight.

for 20 hours. The following day they would be lined up in a cool cellar on stripped pine planks from the nearby sawmill, brushed with a salt solution and turned daily. Later they would be moved to a slightly warmer cellar where the characteristic buff-brown crust would start to form under the watchful eyes – and hands – of the cooperative staff. Then the wheels of cheese would be transferred to the relatively humid *caves d'affinage* (ageing cellars) for final maturing – a minimum of five months, but ideally between one and two years.

At the end of each year a few of that summer's wheels are selected for their suitability for extended ageing, even longer than for regular L'Etivaz. These extra-hard cheeses are called *fromage à rebibes* (*rebibes* are the curly shavings you get from wood-working), and they will come in for special treatment. The rind is cleaned off and the cheeses rubbed with vegetable oil. Then they are stored, lined

The cheesecloth and mould are removed to reveal...

...the newly pressed cheese.

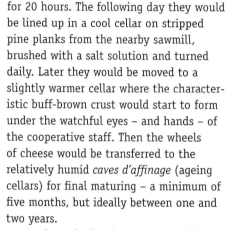

Young cheeses in Claude-Alain's cellar.

The edges are neatened.

There are two different week-long hikes known collectively as Les Chemins du Gruyère which follow the tracks of the mule-drivers of generations ago as they transported the precious Gruyère between the mountains and Lake Geneva. One, Le Chemin de l'Etivaz, starts in Montreux and climbs via Montbovon and Rougemont to the village of l'Etivaz. The other, Le Chemin du Gruyère, starts also in Montreux, climbs to Montbovon, then heads for the hilltop town of Gruyère and finishes in Charmey. Both include visits to alpine cheese makers en route.

For more information contact
Château-d'Oex Tourist Office
Tel. 026 924 25 25
www.chateau-doex.ch

Chemin du Gruyère

up on their sides to permit maximum circulation of air around them, for at least another 30 months.

I asked Christophe what makes L'Etivaz AOC distinctive. He mentioned first the cows' rich diet of alpine flora which gives complex aromas to the milk and in turn to the cheese. He also evoked the cheese's characteristic, slightly smoky flavour, which comes from the wood fire which crackles and burns and perfumes the whole chalet. "When you taste a piece of L'Etivaz, you should be able to hear the sound of the cowbells and the breeze rustling through the alpine plants!" he concluded with a poetic flourish.

Claude-Alain proud displays his new pressed chees

When summer comes, take a drive (or better still, ride the Golden Pass train) from Spiez along the luminous green Simmental. All along this famous valley, intricately carved, dark-stained wooden chalets embellished with geraniums and precision-stacked log piles are hung with simple, homespun signs advertising Alpkäse. This is the heart of Berner Alpkäse AOC and Berner Hobelkäse AOC country. Whatever else you do in this beautiful part of the Bernese Oberland (hiking, golfing, skiing and people-watching in Gstaad are favourite occupations), treat yourself to a taste of this smallest – but by no means least – of Switzerland's alp cheeses.

Despite its modest size – Berner Alpkäse weighs between 7 and 14 kilos, compared to Gruyère AOC's 35–40 kilos – the cheese packs a powerful punch. *"Rächt chüschtig"* – really spicy – is how cheese maker Ernst Kübli describes it. For over 20 years he's been making cheese between June and early September up at the Horneggli chalet above Saanenmöser. The rest of the year he farms down in the valley and sells his milk to the dairy in Schönried. "Our children always used to spend the summers here on the alp with us," comments his wife Margrit, "it's great for kids – and they learned to help out with the cheese making."

Now they've grown up and moved out but son Erhard is set to return soon to take over summer cheese making up at the chalet. He trained first as a carpenter; now he's studying part-time as a *Bergbauer* (mountain farmer). Meanwhile the kids' sleeping quarters, a picture-postcard, pine-panelled room next to the dairy,

have been given over to B & B guests. The room comes complete with red-and-white checked curtains, a jug of wild flowers on the table and a tabby cat curled up in the corner.

The alp is owned by a local farmer; the Küblis rent the chalet and make the cheese. Most years there are around 30 cows grazing the alp. About half of them belong to the Küblis, the other half to the alp-owner, all of them Simmentalers. "They're a lovely placid breed," comments Ernst with evident affection.

The Chalet Horneggli is a classic Oberland wooden chalet, weathered and darkened by the years, its handsome staircase and first-floor balcony festooned with flowers. From here you get sweeping views down the valley. The five-star hotels and jewellery shops of Schönried and Gstaad seem – indeed are – on another planet. In the front room-cum-dairy-cum-dining room, the milk in the copper cauldron was warming gently over an open fire. "Where are the cows?" we wondered aloud,

The Obersimmental Chalet

The Obersimmentalerhausweg or Obersimmental Chalet Trail is a gorgeous hike along the upper Simmental Valley from Boltigen to Lenk with a special focus on the superbly carved and painted farmhouses all along the way. It's best to take it in two four-hour stretches, from Boltigen to Zweisimmen, and Zweisimmen to Lenk. For more information, go to www.lenk-simmental.ch.

puzzled not to have seen any on our way up the track leading to the chalet. Ernst swung open the wooden door from the dairy to reveal a row of curious white faces with curly topknots, gracefully curved horns, café au lait coats, and tails held high by lengths of string to keep them out of the way during milking.

With the milk in the vat at barely blood heat, Ernst added the starter bacteria. This is the Küblis' own starter culture: from each successive batch of cheese Margrit reserves some whey, which she heat-treats and chills overnight ready for the next batch of cheese. Because the culture is specific to their herd and to this alp, the Küblis' Alpkäse has a unique flavour – every Alpkäse tastes different from its neighbour, one of the things that makes alpine cheese tasting such a voyage of discovery.

Next came the rennet to set the milk, and the curds were cut, stirred and heated. Ernst offered us a little to try. They were squeaky on the teeth, quite rubbery and perfectly tasteless. Strange, we reflected, how these bland little blobs would knit together and be transformed by some wonderful alchemy into a smooth, fragrant cheese with superb, complex aromas. *"D'r Chäs tuet*

ständig schaffe!" ("cheese is constantly at work") commented Ernst with relish.

Once the curds had attained the correct temperature and size ('*Stecknadelkopf-gross*', the size of drawing pin heads, according to the rulebook), Ernst threw open the hinged cast-iron jacket enclosing the vat, which he swung out and away from the fire on a sort of gallows-like pulley.

Together Ernst and Margrit completed the graceful gathering up of the curds into the capacious cheesecloth square, closed the corners, squeezed the cloth into a balloon-like bag and lifted it over to the traditional Bernese wooden *Järb* or mould, settling the curds in snugly and tightening the adjustable cord. The cheeses would be pressed overnight, then brined and finally taken down to the cellar to start their long maturing process.

Besides Berner Alpkäse AOC, Ernst makes the even longer-matured Berner Hobelkäse AOC. *Hobel* means a carpenter's plane, indicating the wafer-thin slices that are 'planed' off the cheese using a special mandoline-like slicer. The cheese making process is identical for both Alp and Hobelkäse. Both kinds are then brushed with salt solution and turned regularly for their first few weeks.

Alpkäse is ready for sale after six months' maturing in naturally cool, damp cellars or store rooms (*Spycher*), which must take place in the Berner Alpkäse AOC designated area.

For Hobelkäse, some wheels of the finest (*Surchoix*) quality are singled out for special treatment. The rind is cleaned off (as for L'Etivaz *fromage à rebibes*, page 45) and the wheels moved to a slightly warmer, considerably drier storage room where they will be aged for at least six months more, and up to three years in total. This long

Rolls of Hobelkäse with the Hobel or plane, used for cutting wafer-thin slices.

Ernst and Margrit lifting
the curds.

Ernst pats the curd in place in
its wooden mould.

The official Berner Alpkäse label with the
üblis' identity number.

Wheels of ripe Hobelkäse.

Ernst and Margrit Kübli, notice his shirt made of the Edelweiss fabric shown on the cover of this book. For more information about this fabric, see page 254.

affinage results in an extra-hard cheese with tight structure and powerfully developed flavour.

We settled around the stripped pine table for a tasting of Ernst's one year-old Alpkäse and three year-old Hobelkäse. Both were redolent of the stable and overlaid with faint but unmistakeable hints of wood smoke. The sliced Alpkäse, with a smattering of pea-sized holes and a scattering of crunchy, salty crystals, was pleasingly piquant. The super-fine, almost transparent sheets of the more matured Hobelkäse, rolled into cannelloni-like cylinders, were intensely spicy, the wafer thin sheets melting on the tongue and leaving a deep, long-lasting flavour. Served with gnarled bread from a wood-fired oven, home-made jam and lashings of thick cream skimmed straight from the milk, and accompanied by soothing, warm, bovine smells and a gentle symphony of cowbells from the stable next door, they made a breakfast to remember.

A breakfast to remember: Hobelkäse, coffee and thick cream.

Ernst and Margrit Kübli
Chalet Horneggli
3777 Saanenmöser BE

Tel. 033 744 13 80 or 079 656 46 33

← p. 54/55
'Glacier Superieur du Grindelwald' with the round-log refuge hut.

Cowbells hangin against the chale

Sbrinz AOC

Mention the name Sbrinz even among seasoned cheese-lovers and you may get a blank look. Yet this magnificent golden-rinded, extra-hard cheese has a long and illustrious history. Records show that from the Middle Ages the cheese was the object of lively trade across the Alps, between its *Heimat* (homeland) in the area around Lake Lucerne and its chief export market in northern Italy.

The traffic in Sbrinz was so well established that it followed its own well-worn route through the Alps, which is now known as the Via Sbrinz. From around Stans on the lake the route went south, with a little side step to Brienz, which served as a major assembly point for all the cheese made in the surrounding alps, and which may have given its name to the cheese. (To this day, many local people slip an 'e' into their pronunciation of Sbrinz, so that it sounds like 'Sbrienz'.) From Brienz it continued south along the Haslital and over the Grimsel Pass into the Valais and finally through the Griess Pass to Domodossola, whence the cheeses were

despatched to Lombardy and Piedmont. Eighteenth-century engravings show precarious processions of sumpters (*Säumer*) following the famous route, their animals laden with cheeses snugly stored in special wooden barrels called *Spalen* or *Lagel*, wending their way over bridges straddling swollen torrents below.

I'd always been aware of this extra-hard, grana-type cheese – of the same family as Parmiggiano Reggiano and Grana Padano – but I'd never given Sbrinz much

The Sbrinz route

Keen walkers and/or cheese-lovers with an interest in ancient pathways in the Alps can follow the Sbrinz route for themselves: each year in August, a caravan of latter-day *Säumer*, seasoned hikers and sundry hangers-on retrace this ancient alpine way over a period of about a week. Visit www.sbrinz-route.ch for dates and stopping places.

Andreas Gut, alpine
Sbrinz Meister.

thought beyond its use as a grating cheese, good for gratins and cheese sauces. My first discovery was that this robustly flavoured and textured cheese is well able to stand on its own, delicious for nibbling on reflectively with a glass of wine.

The second revelation, thanks to Swiss cheese specialist Rolf Beeler, was that Sbrinz AOC, like Gruyère, has an alpine sibling. Nine out of the 30 small-scale, artisanal Sbrinz producers make Alp-Sbrinz in the mountain pastures above the lake, and only during the summer months. "Go and see Andreas Gut above Dallenwil in canton Nidwalden," urged Beeler.

I made a date and set off from Stans on the road towards Engelberg. Half an hour later, mildly giddy from numerous hairpin bends ("*Kurvenreich*" – rich in curves – was how the cheese maker had described it on the phone), I drew up in front of the Alpkäserei Chünern, wreathed in early autumn mist. Here, between approximately 20 May and the end of September, Andreas makes his alpine Sbrinz AOC.

The dairy, just across the yard from the farmhouse where the cheese maker lives with his wife and six children, is small and agreeably steamy this cool September morning. Ruddy-faced and moustachioed, Andreas greets us jovially. Cheerful Swiss country music blares out of a battered old radio perched on a windowsill.

In the vat, the milk – sourced from eight farmers nearby – has been acidified by the special Sbrinz culture and thickened by the rennet to a smooth, trembling mass. Andreas slots the cheese harps into place and sets them in motion to cut the curd. The curds are transferred to stainless steel drums where they are heated and stirred constantly. Once they reach the correct temperature, they're transferred to a waiting line of stainless steel, perforated drums that will shape the cheese. Rivers of warm whey course out of the bottom of the moulds, steam rises, the curds are pressed, mechanically rotated and pressed again. Even in this small, simple dairy, wherever possible the cheese-making process is automated so that Andreas can work entirely alone.

After 24 hours the pressing will be complete and the cheeses ready for their salt bath. The salting process for Sbrinz AOC is significantly longer than for other

←p. 60/61
A nineteenth-century lithography depicts a precarious procession making its way through the Grimselpass.

hard cheeses: 20 days in brine as against a mere 24 hours for Gruyère AOC or Emmentaler AOC. This extended brining ensures the good keeping qualities necessary for a long-matured cheese such as Sbrinz AOC, which is aged a minimum of 18 months and anything up to five years.

For the final step before its long affinage, Andreas's Sbrinz spends six weeks in its own private spa – a rather warm, damp cellar. Here the buttery-yellow cheese sweats out excess fat through the rind and is turned twice a week, brushed and gently massaged. During the ripening process the cheese, which started out at around 44 kilos, will lose about 4 kilos in weight.

Sepp Gut, owner of the Käserei Hof in the village of Buochs on Lake Lucerne, is more representative of Sbrinz AOC production today. The cheese-making procedure is broadly the same as for alp cheese, but more automated and on a much larger scale. Sepp buys his milk from 25 farmers within a 5-kilometre radius of the dairy and makes 11 cheeses a day throughout the year (Andreas's total annual production is just 400 wheels, made in summer only). The starter bacteria comes from a specialist lab and the rennet, normally obtained from the stomach of a calf, is micro-biologically produced and animal-free so as to be acceptable to vegetarians.

The maturing of Sepp's deep yellow cheeses starts in the cellar of the Käserei Hof, where they're lined up on their sides, looking like gleaming gold bars, for four months before they are sold on to a wholesaler. Sbrinz AOC is released on the market after a minimum of 18 months but for a fully developed taste treat, Sepp recommends seeking out Sbrinz that's at least two years old.

Attempts to slice Sbrinz are almost certainly doomed to failure – it's too hard.

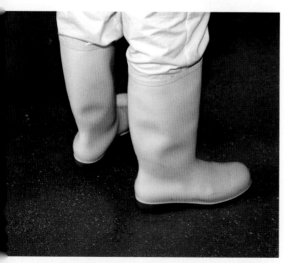

The obligatory white cheese makers' boots.

Attempts to slice Sbrinz are doomed to failure –
use the special Sbrinz chisel to cut chunky flakes.

Instead, you need to use a special Sbrinz
chisel (a bit like the tool used for shuck-
ing oysters) or the point of a small, stocky
knife, and hew the cheese into chunky
flakes, letting it follow its own natural
fault lines. Alternatively, shave it wafer-
thin with a cheese parer or swivel-bladed
potato peeler and scatter it over a salad or
pasta.

Sepp Gut

Schabziger

Approved in 1463 by the local parliament in Glarus, Schabziger is one of the earliest protected brands.

Schabziger, also known as sapsago (or by the brand name Sap Sago in the US), is a curious little conical cheese from canton Glarus. Its greenish tint and intense flavour are due to the addition of a pungent, clover-like herb named *Trigonella Melilotus-caerulea* or blue fenugreek. Something of an acquired taste, Schabziger works well when partnered with pasta, potatoes or rice, or blended with soft butter to make a spread for bread or biscuits, or mixed into fondue. It is one of Switzerland's oldest cheeses, first made in the eighth century in the monasteries of Glarus. Its composition (skimmed cow's milk, lactic acid culture, salt, and blue fenugreek) and its characteristic conical shape have not changed in centuries: the recipe was first formally laid down and approved by the Landsgemeinde (local parliament) of Glarus in 1463, along with the obligatory stamp of origin, making it one of the earliest protected brands. Today, Schabziger is made exclusively by GESKA in Glarus.

The herb blue fenugreek that gives Schabziger its special flavour is cultivated in Glarus.

Geska AG
Glarner Schabziger
Ygrubenstrasse 9
8750 Glarus GL

Tel. 055 640 17 34
www.geska.ch
info@geska.ch

MORE HARD AND EXTRA-HARD CHEESES

Caprinello
Willi Schmid
Städtlichäsi Lichtensteig
Farbgasse 3
9620 Lichtensteig SG

Schwyzer
Herbert Annen
Käserei
Hofstatt 3
6422 Steinen SZ

Fromage des Forts
Michel Beroud
Fromagerie Fleurette
1659 Rougemont VD

Splügen Felsenkeller
Jürg Flükiger
Sennerei Genossenschaft
7435 Splügen GR

Hornbacher, der kleine Berner
Michael Spycher
Käserei Fritzenhaus
3457 Wasen im Emmental BE

Swiss Q
Peter Vogel
Vogel Käsehandwerk GmbH
Käsereistrasse 2
8577 Schönholzerswilen TG

Montagne du Jura
Joseph Spielhofer
Fromages Spielhofer SA
rue de l'Envers 16
2610 St-Imier BE

Toggenburger Bio-Blumenkäse
Thomas Stadelmann
Käserei Stofel
9657 Unterwasser SG

Samnauner Bergkäse
Sennerei Samnaun
Talstrasse 17
7563 Samnaun GR

Urchiger Entlebucher
George Hofstetter
Spezialitäten Käserei
Doppleschwand AG
Dorf
6112 Doppleschwand LU

SEMI-HARD CHEESES

Semi-hard cheeses, which include well-known names such as Appenzeller and Raclette, are the largest branch of the Swiss cheese family. They're moister and more supple than hard cheeses, a direct result of the fact that they are heated to a lower temperature than 'cooked' hard cheeses and the curds less finely cut. They are also subjected to less pressure and matured for just a few months, rarely more than a year.

During their *affinage* they're carefully groomed, regularly turned and brushed with brine or an aromatic solution based on wine, beer, cider, herbs or spices. Thanks to their low melting point, semi-hard cheeses are perfect for cooking. Apart from contributing to fondues or raclette feasts, they can be pressed into service for cheese on toast or sincronizadas (for recipe see page 214). The best of them make fine contributions to the cheese board, flanked by a selection of hard and soft cheeses.

•

Appenzeller

The sun was barely up over the snow-dusted fields when I arrived early one winter's morning at the small dairy in Schachen near Heiden, in Appenzell's easternmost corner. Cheese maker Marcel Tobler was waiting outside. "Jump in," he said, indicating a white van with a small, integrated milk tanker parked outside the back door, "we're going to fetch some milk."

We roared out of the village up a snowy track and came to a halt outside a long, low farmhouse. The young farmer, Guido Geiger, and his father, both in overalls, stout boots and tasselled woolly hats, eyed us warily as we crunched across the yard. They'd expected Marcel – he comes every morning to fetch the milk fresh from their 45-strong herd of Brown Swiss cows; what they hadn't reckoned with was a notebook-wielding food writer and a camera-touting photographer. "I'm off to get changed," joked Guido's father. "I can't take a picture of you in a suit" countered Niko, the photographer – "no-one's going to believe it!" After a bit of persuasion they both agreed to be photographed in working gear and we were invited inside to meet the cows.

The Geigers, father and son in their working gear.

As we entered the barn, 42 pairs of soulful brown eyes swivelled round in our direction. Then the cows resumed munching their breakfast rations of hay. They looked the picture of Swiss health, beautifully kempt and groomed as if ready for the show ring. Behind them, the milking parlour was spotless, the floor freshly sluiced down now that milking was complete, the churns, hoses and sundry milking paraphernalia all sparkling clean. For Marcel, whose Appenzeller is made from raw milk, scrupulous hygiene is essential at every stage of the cheese-making process – and the cheese-making process starts at the farm.

Back at the dairy Marcel piped this latest batch of milk through to the large, stainless steel, domed vat. We donned protective overalls, hairnets and shoe coverings and joined Marcel's mum, who assists with the daily cheese making. Like most small cheese dairies in Switzerland, this is a family business.

The by-now familiar programme swung into action, the milk was gently warmed, the culture and rennet were added, the milky mass was slashed and sliced into small pieces ("half the size of corn kernels") by the rotating cheese harps, heated and pumped over to a line of tall plastic moulds. The curds would now be pressed and the cheeses date-stamped before going into brine for a couple of days.

It's at this moment that the wheels of Appenzeller, which typically weigh about 7 kilos and measure about 30 cm across, come in for some rather special grooming. During their first two weeks in the cellar, Marcel or his assistant Hans-Jörg regularly turn, brush and smear the cheeses with an

A snowy scene in Appenzell.

aromatic solution which helps not only to build the rusty-brown crust but also gives the typical spicy Appenzeller flavour. I asked what goes into the mixture. There was a sharp intake of breath, lips were pursed, eyes averted. Its exact composition, it seems, is a closely guarded secret (though herbs, spices, wine and salt are admitted to play a part). Apart from adding an element of mystery, this smearing of the rind confers on Appenzeller its unique flavour. Of all the semi-hard cheeses, it's probably the one with the most muscular flavour.

Once Marcel's cheeses have been aged between 20 and 40 days, he sells them on to an Appenzeller wholesaler specialised in completing the ripening process. It's the wholesaler's decision which of the wheels will be aged three months (*Classic*) and which will mature for at least

four (*Surchoix*). Some wheels are selected for ripening six months or more (*Extra*). Most pungent of all is Appenzeller Räss, a low-fat version which is smeared and ripened for at least eight months. While Appenzeller is a firm favourite on its home turf, it has also captured a creditable slice of the export market: about 60 per cent

Brown Swiss cows eye us curiously.

← p. 72/73
As hard as the work of cheese making is, this nineteenth century painting of a cheese maker in Appenzell makes it look as if it could be fun for the whole family.

of production is sold outside Switzerland, principally in Germany.

Throughout the morning, a steady stream of faithful customers appeared at the back door to buy Marcel's prize-winning Appenzeller – it was awarded a gold medal in the 2009 Mountain Cheese Olympics. Frau Tobler sliced off some finger-sized pieces of *Surchoix* for us to sample. Intensively coached by now in the art of cheese-tasting, we admired first its small, evenly spaced holes, bent it approvingly over into a rainbow shape, sniffed its deliciously robust farmyard aromas and finally savoured its rich, spicy taste.

Marcel Tobler with his prize-winning cheese.

Marcel Tobler
Käserei Tobler
Schachen 162
9414 Schachen bei Reute AR

Tel. 071 891 16 62
marcel-tobler@bluewin.ch
www.kaeserei-tobler.ch

p. 76/77→
An Appenzeller farming family exchanges secrets on the maturing process for their cheese – the farmer in the centre wears the traditional tasselled cap, typical of Appenzell Inner-Rhoden.

Tête de Moine AOC

Originally made by the monks at the beautiful Benedictine monastery of Bellelay in the Jura mountains, this chunky little cylinder of cheese was first chronicled in 1192 and known for several centuries simply as Bellelay cheese. Its present name, Tête de Moine, appeared only about the time of the French Revolution. Today, it is made in nine dairies dotted throughout the Jura mountain region.

For a taste of Tête de Moine AOC, pack a picnic and head for the hills – specifically for the area in the Jura known as les Franches Montagnes, close to where the cheese is typically made. The landscape is wild and beautiful and only moderately steep (in the Jura you're rarely higher than 1000 metres), dotted with tall, erect Norway Spruces, their branches sweeping low to the ground. In the lush, close-cropped meadows, countless free-ranging, toffee-coloured Freiberger horses with crew-cut black manes graze peaceably together with the cows whose milk goes to make the famous cheese.

Here you'll be well placed for a post-picnic visit to any of the nine Tête de Moine AOC dairies in the neighbourhood (see www.tetedemoine.ch for a list and map of producers). The Fromagerie Spielhofer in the watchmaking town of St Imier provides a friendly and informative visit. It's a family business, founded by the Spielhofer parents some 20 years ago and employs 16 staff including the two Spielhofer sons, Cédric and Florian. They make several different cheeses including Mont-Soleil, Eolienne – named after the wind turbine on the hill – and Erguel. But their award-winning Tête de Moine AOC is the great classic, and the one of which they're especially proud.

Every morning a team of helpers fans out to collect the milk from between 50 and 60 hill farms dotted around St Imier and brings it back to the dairy. The milk comes exclusively from pastured animals; silage is strictly forbidden as it can taint the milk, interfere with the cheese-making process and affect the flavour. July, August and September are the chief months for making Tête de Moine AOC, not so much because the milk is particularly rich and fragrant during these summer months (which it is), but because the cheeses made in summer will be ready just in time for Christmas – a peak period for serving up this lovely, spicy cheese.

A specific Tête de Moine starter bacteria is added to the raw milk along with the rennet. Once coagulated, the curds are cut, heated and stirred, then shovelled into small perforated moulds and the copious whey is drained off. You need between 8 and 11 litres of milk to arrive at one tiny Tête de Moine AOC cheese, which typically weighs 700–900g – the rest is whey. (Throughout Switzerland there are lots of chubby pigs and calves, fattened on oceans of whey, the relentless by-product of cheese making.)

Next the cheeses are pressed, salted and finally matured in the cellar for a minimum of 75 days. "I like them best when they've had 90 days at least" admits Cédric Spielhofer, "then the flavours have really had time to develop!"

Tête de Moine AOC is served cut or shaved into the characteristic frilly rosettes. For this you need a Girolle® (pictured on page 83), a special cheese-

Woodcut showing the typical Jura farmhouses, horses and cows grazing in the meadows and majestic Norway spruces behind.

paring instrument with a central spindle on which the cheese is impaled. Onto this is slotted a horizontal blade that you wind round and round over the surface of the cheese to shave off the typical curls. What if you don't eat Tête de Moine regularly and don't want to invest in a Girolle? There are two solutions, according to Cédric: buy the newly patented disposable cheese parer called a Pirouette, designed by Olivier Isler of the Tête de Moine AOC producers association, and sold in kit form complete with a half-cheese, or simply shave or pare off slivers of cheese from the top using a cheese parer or vegetable peeler.

The point, insists Cédric, is to cut paper-thin slices, however best you can achieve them. This allows those layers of spicy flavour to unfold on the tongue. *"Ça nous fait mal au coeur"* ("it really pains us"), he remarks ruefully, "when people cut Tête de Moine in segments and munch on great thick chunks – they just don't get the full flavour!"

The cheese maker checks that the curd is ready to be pumped over to the perforated moulds.

The tops of the filled moulds are smoothed.

In former times thin slices of Tête de Moine were pared off the top of the cheese using a sharp knife, until Nicolas Crevoisier, a precision engineer from Canton Jura, devised the Girolle (pictured above). The design was patented in 1981 and proved a resounding success. Over 2.5 million have been sold to date. To the delight of Tête de Moine producers, sales of the spicy little cheese also took off, thanks to this convenient way of producing the famous curly rosettes.

Fromagerie Spielhofer
Rue de l'Envers 16
2610 St-Imier BE

Tel. 032 940 17 44
info@fromagesspielhofer.ch
www.fromagesspielhofer.ch

Vacherin Fribourgeois AOC

Vacherin Fribourgeois AOC is a medium-sized, semi-hard cheese with an orangey-brown rind, typically combined with Gruyère in the classic *moitié-moitié* ('half-and-half') fondue. Its name is related to the Latin *vaccarinus*, meaning 'little cowhand'. According to the strict hierarchy of alpine cheese making, the *maître-armailli* or master herdsman and chief cheese maker was the one who got to make Gruyère. Beneath him in the pecking order was the *petit vacherin* or *bouébo* (in Fribourg patois), the junior cowhand, who was allowed to make a smaller cheese which was known, by association with its maker, as Vacherin. It's often described as Gruyère's kid brother, because the two tend to grow up together in the same dairy. Big brother Gruyère averages 35 kilos while Vacherin Fribourgeois weighs a mere 6–10 kilos.

Like all of Switzerland's traditional cheeses, Vacherin Fribourgeois AOC was originally made in small alpine chalets and in summer only. When cheese making moved from the alpine pastures down into the lowlands in the nineteenth century, Vacherin began to be made in village dairies throughout canton Fribourg. At first production was confined mainly to the autumn and winter months, whose cooler temperatures provided ideal conditions for the maturing cheeses. Nowadays, Vacherin Fribourgeois AOC is made all year round.

Many people dismiss the familiar, semi-hard cheese with holes as something to put in fondue because it melts nicely. It's true that thanks to its low melting point (around ten degrees lower than Gruyère's or Emmentaler's), Vacherin Fribourgeois AOC gives you that smooth, fondant quality long before it overheats and turns into telegraph wires or – worse – chewing gum.

But it's a shame to confine Vacherin Fribourgeois AOC to the fondue pot; instead, give it a chance to shine on the cheese board. Those who know and love this cheese insist that there are huge variations in flavour from one dairy to another; it all depends who made it – the famous *main du fromager* or cheese maker's hand. Because of these local variations – the cheesy equivalent of *terroir* in wine – it's worth shopping around and tasting widely. Look out too for Vacherin Fribourgeois d'alpage, the summer cheese made in the Prealps of canton Fribourg from raw milk. These are cheeses with real attitude, with unruly, dark brown crusts and full, frank, barnyard flavours.

I emailed Louis Bérard, *artisan fromager* in Chavannes-les-Forts, between Bulle and Romont, to seek enlightenment on these subtle differences. By return, he replied graciously that with the greatest of pleasure he would help me to discover *"les charmes bucoliques"* of his own particular farmhouse Vacherin Fribourgeois.

The real Vacherin Fribourgeois

Unless you live in or near Fribourg, you'll probably be restricted to bog-standard, plastic-wrapped Vacherin Fribourgeois, fine for fondue but a pale shadow of the cheese at its fragrant best. For a good selection that shows Vacherin in all its astonishing variety, try to find a cheese shop that stocks several different kinds including an alpine Vacherin, and treat yourself to a tasting.

FONDUE

The tradition of cheese melted with wine dates back many centuries – Homer's *Iliad* has a 'sauce' consisting of white wine and grated goat's cheese. Fondue has traditionally been made throughout Switzerland wherever cheese is made and where wine is grown, and almost every Swiss canton is keen to claim parentage of what is now considered the national dish.

It was in the 1950s that fondue really began to take off in Switzerland. It provided the perfect answer to the problem of over-production of cheese sanctioned by the Swiss Cheese Union: if they could persuade people to eat 150–200g (5–7 oz) of cheese per person once a week in the form of fondue, went the reasoning, the cheese mountain would be whittled away and the battle half won. A famous advertising campaign to incite the Swiss to ever greater fondue feats claimed that the dish was not only good but moreover would put you in a good mood – in Swiss German: *Fondue isch guet und git e gueti Luune*, popularly shortened to '*figugegl*'.

The idea soon spread beyond Switzerland's borders and by the 1960s, a fondue set with earthenware pan (known in both French and German as a *caquelon*), spirit burner and brightly coloured forks for spearing the bread cubes had become an almost obligatory wedding present to British and American brides.

As to which cheeses to put in fondue, there are few hard and fast rules – at least none that are universally agreed upon. Probably the best known is the so-called *moitié/moitié* (half-and-half) from canton Fribourg, which contains equal quantities of Swiss Gruyère AOC and Vacherin Fribourgeois AOC.

Every Swiss region favours its own cheese: in the Jura you might get a mixture of Tête de Moine and Gruyère, in central Switzerland Sbrinz will certainly play a part together with some semi-hard, melting cheese, while in eastern Switzerland the logical choice will be a combination of Appenzeller and Tilsiter. The recipe on page 210 gives plenty of scope for creativity in composing your own Swiss cheese fondue.

An earthenware pan is always used (keep metal pans for meat fondues), in which the grated cheese is gently melted with crushed garlic and white wine, lightly thickened with cornflour (cornstarch) and flavoured with nutmeg, freshly ground pepper and maybe a shot of Kirsch. Tradition dictates that it is essential to stir the pot continuously with a wooden fork in a figure of eight to ensure a perfectly smooth result. At table, cubes of crusty bread are the classic dipping material (though button mushrooms and bite-sized cooked peeled potatoes are also permissible). Each cube of bread must have a side of crust, otherwise it will fall off the fork into the pan. If this happens, a forfeit, agreed on by the fondue participants, will be levied. As the fondue nears its conclusion, a delectable golden crust will start to form in the base of the pan. This is *la réligieuse*, also known as *la croûte*, a kind of lacy cheese crisp which should be prised off and carefully divided up amongst participants.

A final tip: the pan should be filled with cold water after using, so that the remains of melted cheese do not harden and stick to the bottom.

E' guete/bon appétit/buon appetito/bun appetit!

Grand-père Bérard was the first to make cheese at the village Laiterie on the main street of Chavannes-les-Forts in 1935 and the tenancy has passed down from father to son ever since. Nowadays, the Bérards work with 15 milk producers all within reach of the village. Most of their Vacherin – indeed almost all Vacherin Fribourgeois AOC – is made with thermised milk. Bérard readily acknowledges that this changes the flavour – "the product is milder, more homogenous," he says, "it's also easier to control, and you get a more even result, one that you can replicate all year round." During the winter months he makes a small proportion with raw milk – "*pour la vente locale*" (for local sale). Both raw and thermised milk are permitted under the rules of the Vacherin Fribourgeois AOC, created in 2005.

On a sunny winter's day Louis Bérard shows a sunny cheese with a sunny smile.

The recipe is the familiar one for semi-hard cheese. First the starter cultures, selected from a list approved by the Vacherin Fribourgeois AOC consortium, are added to the thermised, cooled milk. Renneting follows, and the curd is cut and stirred until, in Bérard's words, the grains are "somewhere between the size of a hazelnut and a grain of wheat." Then the curds are heated, pressed, drained and brined for just 12 hours (compared to Gruyère's 24 hours, or Sbrinz's 20 days). Maturing, which takes place in the Berards' cellars, takes from three to six months "*selon les gouts*" ("according to taste"). Some of the cheeses are fully matured on the premises, for sale in the dairy shop in Chavannes. The rest goes to an *affineur* who completes the ageing.

When I ask Monsieur Bérard what is the optimal age for Vacherin Fribourgeois, he responds gallantly: "*tous les ages ont leur charme!*" ("all ages have their charm") adding that it all depends on when you want to eat it, and with what. The younger, milder cheeses are fine as part of a typically Swiss breakfast spread, while the longer-aged or alpine ones are delicious as 'dessert cheese' (at the end of a meal). For cooking, apart from its use in the classic fondue (either in combination with Gruyère or all Vacherin, with cheeses at various stages of ripeness), Vacherin works beautifully on top of a *croûte au fromage* (cheese on toast, Swiss-style).

True to tradition, Monsieur Bérard produces both Gruyère and Vacherin in the same dairy. Historically, he explains, "we've always made more Vacherin – but both of them have their place in our hearts. They're part of our *patrimoine* (heritage), which we want to pass on to future generations."

Cats laze in the sun, awaiting a saucer of milk from the dairy.

Louis Bérard
Laiterie
Route d'Oron 116
1676 Chavannes-les-Forts FR

Tel. 026 656 13 42
louis.berard@bluewin.ch
www.terroir-fribourg.ch/
modules/catalog/contact.asp?ID=16026

Piora formaggio d'alpe ticinese DOP

Alpine cheese making high up in the startlingly beautiful, sun-bathed Val Piora above Quinto near the Gotthard Pass has an ancient and venerable history. A statute dated 25 May 1227 in Quinto defining owner-ship and grazing rights is proof that the unique nature of this rich, 3500-hectare alpine valley was already highly prized in the thirteenth century. According to the statute, the Piora alp was to be owned and administered by a *Corporazione di Boggesi*, a cooperative of herdsmen whose cattle were entitled to graze up on the alp dur-ing the summer months.

To this day, descendants of the original Boggesi continue to enjoy these rights. Some of them still farm in the commune of Quinto, in which case they may send their cows up for summer grazing, subject (as in all alpine pastures) to an overall ceiling that limits the number of beasts on the alp each season. Even non-farming descendants (nowadays they're bankers or dentists, or expatriate Swiss living in Chile or Ecuador) still have the right to send up one cow each. And cows, in this context, mean cheese – the famously fragrant and ferociously expensive Piora which is made here and distributed amongst the members of the Corporazione at the end of summer.

A nineteenth-century view of Airolo from the south side of the Gotthard Pass – the Alpe Piora is high up to the right.

Canton Ticino has around 80 *alpeggi* (alpine pastures) where cheese is made. Of these, around 30 have applied for and received the *Denominazione d'Origine Protetta* (see Glossary, page 244). Alpine cheeses are always more expensive than their lowland cousins, but the price that Ticinese alp cheeses command (typically about double that of Gruyère d'alpage, for example) brings tears to the eyes of envious cheese-making colleagues north of the Gotthard and guarantees cheeses such as Piora a place on any aspirational cheese board.

Such a cheese, such promise! I felt a visit to Piora's homeland coming on. From Signor Adriano Dolfini, secretary of the Corporazione di Boggesi, I learnt that access to the alp by car is restricted. The obvious solution seemed to be Switzerland's superbly joined-up public transport system, which reaches parts that other transport systems can only dream of. Travelling by train, post bus, funicular and on foot I could be up in the Val Piora from Basel in time for supper. All I needed was somewhere to sleep on the alp, since cheese making always requires an early start.

I enlisted my friend Alwyn to join me on the adventure and booked us both in at the Capanna Cadagno, a mountain refuge five minutes from the *caseificio*

Lago Ritom, on the way to the Alpe Piora.

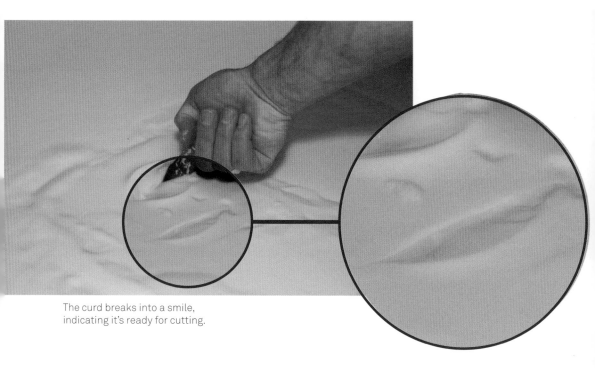

The curd breaks into a smile,
indicating it's ready for cutting.

(dairy). We packed rucksacks and boarded the train in Basel. Outside Airolo station, the post bus to Piotta awaited and from there it was a short walk to the foot of the Ritom funicular. We soared up, marvelling at the view of the valley below. At the top we found a few thirsty hikers seated at trestle tables outside a small café, downing evening glasses of beer to the strains – appropriately – of 'Knock, knock, knockin' on heaven's door.'

We struck out towards the refuge in glorious evening sunshine, skirting the Lago Ritom, like a huge, deep blue infinity pool with its dam at one end and a range of distant peaks beyond. An hour later we reached the simple, stone-built Capanna Cadagno, 1987 metres above sea level.

Tired, happy and gleefully anticipating the next cheesy adventure, we installed ourselves on the terrace outside the Capanna within sight of the *caseificio*. Over an epic supper of *manzo brasato* (braised beef) and crunchy, corny polenta, we were treated to front-row-of-the-stalls views of the dying sun as it sank below the jagged peaks to the west. As dusk gathered, we heard a chorus of cowbells, shouts, whistles and barking dogs beneath us, as the grey-brown cows were herded out of the dairy after the evening milking and up the track to spend the night on the alp.

At 8.30 next morning, Signor Dolfini arrived to escort us to the dairy, where cheese makers Paolo Alberti and his helper Filippo had already made a start. Paolo dipped the familiar dustpan-like plastic shovel deeply into the coagulated milk and raised it gently, experimentally to the surface. *"Deve fare il sorriso!"* he said, "it has to smile." Obligingly the curd broke open into a wide grin, indicating that it was ready to be cut, heated and stirred.

The Caseificio or mountain dairy where Piora cheese is made.

Paolo, originally from Bergamo in northern Italy, has worked on the Piora alp every summer for the past 12 years. Photographs displayed on the wall in a small parlour next door show how the cheese used to be made – in a simple, kitchen-like room in the classic copper vats heated over a wood fire, with the curds scooped up in huge squares of cheesecloth, drained of their whey and patted into moulds.

In 2004 the whole Piora cheese-making operation shifted into another gear. A state-of-the-art *caseificio* was built, consisting of two long, low stone buildings with slate roofs, their architecture entirely in sympathy with the rugged alpine landscape. One is the milking parlour for the 240-odd cows, the other is the cheese dairy. It's an impressively high-tech, stainless steel affair, bristling with taps, valves, hoses and hydraulic aids for processing the vast quantities of milk and cheese.

How did Paolo manage the transition from the old regime to the new? "*Il primo anno – mamma mia!!*" he moans, smacking his forehead with the palm of his hand as he recalls his first year in the new dairy, "so many pipes, so many taps!" In 2006 the Corporazione's massive investment was rewarded, when 49 Ticino alpine cheeses – including Piora – gained the coveted Denominazione d'Origine Protetta or DOP (see Glossary, page 244).

Now Paolo seems entirely at home in his surroundings, activating the harps to cut the curd into small granules, raising the temperature to heat the curds, connecting hoses to pump them over into tall, straight-sided moulds, pressing and turning the cheeses. The final step, trimming the edges of the formed cheeses with a sort of dough scraper before they go down into the cellar to their salt bath, is about the only remaining manual part of what has become a highly mechanised, automated operation.

At the end of the season – from 65–75 days long, between June and September, depending on the weather and the state of the grass – the cheeses are totted up and the year's production (average: around 2700 cheeses) is tabulated laboriously in felt-tip pen on a homespun board hanging in the cellar. Later the precious, greyish-brown Piora cheeses are distributed amongst the Boggesi. The number they are allotted is directly related to how many cows they had on the alp, and the cows' milk yield – it works out at roughly ten cheeses per cow. The owners are then free to dispose of the precious wheels at will. With the kind of prices Piora fetches, it must be tempting to sell at least some to *affineurs* or restaurants, provided the cheeses are aged at least 60 days, in line with the DOP regulations. But a few will certainly be kept back for private savouring with selected friends.

Hi-tech cheese pressing.

Down in the valley once more, we found we'd missed our post bus connection and the next one was not due for over an hour. A charming resident of Piotta, on her way back from tending her allotment, took pity on us and gave us a lift to Airolo station ten minutes away. We regaled her with our Piora adventures. "Ayyyy," she breathed, raising her eyes to the mountains above, "*il famoso Piora* – sure, it's expensive, but you eat a little bit of that cheese and it's as good as eating a piece of fillet steak!"

Once home, we unpacked our precious cheese and gazed reverently at it. Aged one year, the flesh was a pale, primrose-yellow with a mild rash of pea-sized holes.

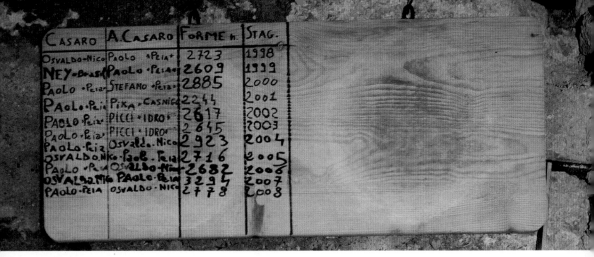

CASARO	A. CASARO	FORME n.	STAG.
Osvaldo-Nico	Paolo •Peia•	2723	1998
NEY-...	Paolo •Peia•	2609	1999
Paolo •Peia•	Stefano •Peia•	2885	2000
Paolo •Peia•	Pika •Casnic	2244	2001
Paolo •Peia•	Picci •Idro•	2617	2002
Paolo •Peia•	Picci •Idro•	2645	2003
Paolo •Peia•	Osvaldo •Nico	2923	2004
Osvaldo Nico	Paolo •Peia•	2716	2005
Paolo •Pei•	Osvaldo Ni	2682	2006
Osvaldo Nic	Paolo •Peia•	3294	2007
Paolo •Peia•	Osvaldo •Nico	2778	2008

The wooden board above shows the name of the cheese maker, his helper, and the number of cheeses year by year.

The precious Pioras are aged on wooden shelves.

We inhaled gentle barnyard aromas and detected faint hints of hay and mushrooms. The flesh was velvety-smooth and melting, the flavour rich, complex and long-lasting.

Was it worth twice as much as other great alpine cheeses? How did the fillet steak analogy hold up? Did the earth move for us? Ruefully, I have to admit that the honest answer would be 'maybe not'. What was priceless, though, was the total Alpe Piora experience. I wouldn't have missed that for the world.

Corporazione di Boggesi
Alpe Piora
c/o Signor Adriano Dolfini
6777 Quinto TI

Tel. 091 868 11 50
Tel. (dairy) 091 868 13 25

Tilsiter

Tilsiter is a soft-spoken cheese, not given to wearing loud ties or throwing its weight about. You'll often hear it described as a *Frühstückskäse* (breakfast cheese), which seems like faint praise, but is actually a fair description. Breakfast, after all, is probably not the moment for challenging cheeses, but rather for meek ones, cut in fine slivers for nibbling with fresh bread, sweet butter, home-made black cherry jam and foaming hot chocolate.

Among Switzerland's classic cheeses, Tilsiter is the new kid on the block, barely 100 years old. The original recipe was not even Swiss. It came from what was then the small town of Tilsit in East Prussia (now Sovetsk in the Russian exclave of Kaliningrad), where it was discovered in 1893 by two wandering cheese makers from Thurgau in eastern Switzerland. Considering that it had potential as a new cheese variety for the Swiss market, they returned home with the recipe, changed the shape from a long loaf to a small wheel and gave the flavour a bit of a boost.

The transplanted, reinterpreted Tilsiter grew steadily in popularity (amongst Switzerland's semi-hard cheeses, it follows Raclette and Appenzeller in quantities produced) and has established a secure place in Swiss affections. It's made in about 30 small dairies scattered throughout the rich farming country bounded by Lake Constance to the north, the Lake of Zurich to the west and Appenzell's Säntis mountain in the east.

Today, there are three types of Swiss Tilsiter: one with a red label, one with yellow and one with green. The tastiest is the red-label variety, made from raw milk. The green and the yellow (with added cream), are made from pasteurised milk, which gives a very bland result. Because the pasteurisation process (see Glossary, page 245) requires special equipment, most Tilsiter dairies specialise, making either the red, raw milk variety or the green and yellow pasteurised types, but not both. About half of all Tilsiter is still made from unpasteurised milk.

This is the case at the Käserei Rüttiberg in Rufi, just north of the Walensee in canton St Gallen, which works only with raw milk – and it was one of the reasons why I chose to visit them. Another was that the cheese maker, Reto Maag, the fourth generation of the Maag family to work in this small village dairy, was recently crowned Tilsiter Champion by his peers in the professional organisation. Also – unusually – he's a young cheese maker (in his mid-twenties), whereas many in this region are nearing retirement.

It was a dark December morning and snowing gently when I drew up in front of the dairy. "I do two batches of cheese every morning," Reto had explained on the phone, "one starts at 6.20, the other

soon after 9.00." I had a mid-morning date with Willi Schmid in Lichtensteig (see page 122) so there was nothing for it but the early shift. "Do we get a *Kaffee-pause?*" (coffee break) I asked wistfully. *"Natürlich!"* came Reto's cheerful reply.

Reto's seven suppliers had just completed delivery of their milk for weighing and checking. The largest, with 45 cows (mainly the moleskin-coloured, doe-eyed Brown Swiss), brings in about 1000 litres in a small tanker towed behind his tractor; the smallest, with just two cows, delivers his 24 litres in churns. All over Switzerland this small-scale delivery of early-morning milk to the village dairy is replicated, with each dairy transforming the same raw material – milk – into a cheese that's unique and special to that dairy and that region.

The Rüttiberg Tilsiter starts out in a big, bathtub-shaped vat with the customary addition of the culture and the rennet. When the milk begins to set, Reto tests the curd, dipping his index finger into the surface and lifting it up so that the curd breaks open, like a smooth slash on the surface of a Lucio Fontana canvas.

Next the curds are cut with harps into rice-sized pieces and the whey begins to take on a greenish-gold cast. Some of the whey is drawn off and Reto hooks a hose over the side of the vat and pumps in a large quantity of water, a step known as

← Throughout Switzerland, in winter and in summer, the early-morning milk is delivered by the farmers by different means direct to the dairy, as captured in this contemporary painting which shows the Steingrube Dairy in canton Bern.

The smoothly set curd before it is cut.

The harps stand ready to cut the curd...

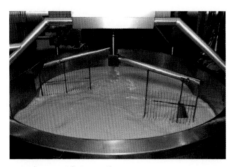

...and are set into motion.

The froth is skimmed off and the whey removed.

'washing the curd' which slows down the frenetic starter bacteria activity and reduces acidity in the finished cheese. With quick, spare, efficient gestures – and some help from his apprentice ("his Dad taught mine; now I'm teaching him") – Reto completes the heating of the curd, pumps it over to the moulds, skims off the froth and allows more whey to drain off. Then he activates the presses. A quarter of an hour later, the formed cheeses are turned, stamped with day's date and the dairy identification number and then pressed for a further ten minutes.

Once formed and pressed, the cheeses are brined for between one and two days, then laid on wooden shelves and brushed and turned daily. Tilsiter is one of the smallest semi-hard cheeses, typically weighing just 4.5 kilos and measuring about 25 cm across, like a large dinner plate. After about two months in Reto's cellar, the cheeses move to the cellars of a wholesaler for their final *affinage*. Red-label Tilsiter comes in two 'strengths': *mittelreif* or *mi-salé*, aged between 70 and 110 days, is the milder of the two; *Surchoix* or *relevé* is matured for up to six months and has a riper, more pronounced flavour.

The promised Kaffeepause turned out to be a full-blown breakfast across the road in Reto's parents' kitchen, with rye bread, coffee, preserves and fragrant slices of Reto's *Surchoix* cheese. What does the future hold, I wondered, for a small village dairy like the Rüttiberg, making a cheese such as Tilsiter often – unfairly – dismissed as a *Frühstückskäse*? "We'll see," says Reto, adding with a smile: "I'm never going to be rich but I can make a decent living and I have a job that I love – not everyone can say that!"

Reto's Surchoix Tilsiter – the red label signifies that the cheese is made from raw milk.

Familie Maag
Käserei Rüttiberg
8723 Rufi SG

....

Tel. 055 615 15 84
maagreto@me.com
www.tilsiter.ch/sortenorganisation/
kaeser/maag-reto.html

Bündner Bergkäse and Bündner Alpkäse

Cheese has been made for centuries in the Alps of Graubünden, as in all of Switzerland's mountain cantons. But while cheese making was historically of major economic importance in other alpine regions, in Graubünden the emphasis was more on cattle farming and breeding than on dairying and cheese making. According to the *Kulinarisches Erbe der Schweiz*, a database of traditional Swiss food products, beef was favoured here, raised both for export and for local consumption. Some of it was certainly destined for Bündnerfleisch, the fragrant, cured, air-dried beef for which Graubünden is justly celebrated.

Over the years dairying and cheese making became more important. Summer cheese making continued in the alpine dairies, but in the nineteenth century the first *Sennereien* (village dairies) were established down in the valleys, where cheese could be made all year round. Other developments followed – the first cantonal dairy school, stricter controls and standardisation of the recipe – all of which helped to improve standards and to put Graubünden on the Swiss cheese map.

Nowadays, Bündner Bergkäse (and its summer sibling Bündner Alpkäse) are made throughout this rugged 'canton of 150 valleys'. Alpkäse remains a summer-only cheese, made in around 130 chalets from the milk

of cows taken up to the high pastures for their annual transhumance. Bergkäse, on the other hand, can in theory be made all year round; in practice, production is often confined to the winter months, using milk from cows stabled down in the village. Thirteen village dairies dotted throughout the canton make Bündner Bergkäse, which is a recognised brand, though not (yet) an AOC (see Glossary page 244).

At the Sennerei in the little village of Ftan, perched above Scuol in the lower Engadine valley, cheese maker Stephan Forrer is one who makes Bergkäse only in winter. Mostly he starts at around 5 a.m. sometimes at 3 a.m. "Why so early?" I asked, anxiously, mentally programming a possible visit. "That way I finish in good time and I can get out onto the ski slopes," he grins. Stephan came here a few years ago from his native canton Fribourg, drawn principally by the offer of a job (he's employed by the eight farmers who supply the dairy with milk), but also by the beauty of this alpine valley and its rich skiing possibilities. Like others who make cheese in mountainous regions, he alternates his duties with a little downhill work and some part-time ski instructing.

As usual in small village dairies the milk comes in twice a day,

delivered in churns or mini-tankers by the farmers who own the dairy. All of them farm organically, so cheese from the *Sennerei* in Ftan is labelled with the Bio-Knospe, the green bud logo used by Switzerland's organic certification body.

Stephan's first task of the day is to thermise the combined evening and morning milk (see Glossary page 245). Then he cools the milk rapidly to lukewarm and adds the specific Bündner Bergkäse culture which will allow the distinctive texture, flavour and character of the cheese to develop. Stephan enumerates the other factors that will influence the final taste of his Ftaner Bergkäse, including how it's made, how and when the salting is done and – crucially – the length of time and the conditions in which it's matured.

Presently he reaches into the vat, dodging the whirling harps, and fishes out a handful of curds to show me how things are progressing. Some pieces are the size of little fingernails (optimal), others are more like thumbnails (too big). The harps complete the curd-cutting till all are of an even size. Right on cue, Stephan offers me some to taste (all cheese makers proffer their curds for a taste test). They're predictably rubbery and squeaky on the teeth, with absolutely no flavour. "That comes later," he reassures me.

Once evenly cut, the curds are heated – not 'cooked' as are hard cheeses which are firmer and drier, but warmed just enough to give the characteristic smooth, melting texture required in semi-hard cheeses. Next Stephan draws off some whey from the vat and replaces it with an equal volume of water. Finally the washed curds are pumped across to a cheese table, like a big rectangular stainless steel trough with draining holes at each corner.

The cheeses are moulded and pressed...

...brushed daily with brine...

...and matured on wooden shelves.

← p. 106/107
Cheese maker Stephan Forrer with Ftan's Gemeinde-Präsident (mayor) who supplies hay for the cows in winter.

The whey seeps off, leaving a great block of curd about a foot (30 cm) deep. The block is pressed en masse and then cut into chunky squares like breeze blocks (cinder blocks).

Working in tandem, Stephan and his helper lift out the firmly set but biddable squares of curd and drop them, one by one, into the circular stainless steel perforated moulds, squashing them in firmly so they assume the shape of the mould. The newly formed cheeses are subjected to mounting pressure for about an hour, after which they'll spend 24 hours in brine. Finally the cheeses will be moved to the cellar where there will be periodic turnings and brushings with brine to draw out more moisture and encourage formation of the rind. Stephan takes us down to the cool, clammy cellar to check out the cheeses. We're assaulted by a pervasive smell of ammonia. The eye-watering, nose-wrinkling smell, which in finished cheese is an indication that it's overripe and probably only good for the bin, is par for the course for young cheese that's in the process of maturing, explains Stephan. He cuts a sliver from a one-month old wheel for us to sample. It's meek, mild and gently creamy – definitely a breakfast cheese. The one year-old Bergkäse is more muscular, with well developed haybarn flavours and a nice mountain bite.

The Ftan dairy has a contract with the Migros supermarket chain, which takes on the cheeses after their initial three-week ripening at the dairy and completes the maturing process. When the cheeses have aged at least three months, they're despatched to shops throughout the country. You can't buy cheese direct from the dairy but a small amount is sold locally in the little Volg village stores all along the Engadine valley.

Sennerei Ftan
7551 Ftan GR

Tel. 081 864 94 75

p. 110/111 →
A goatherd tends his goats close to the Rheinwald glacier, the highest point on the San Bernardino transalpine sumpters' route.

Raclette

R aclette is a semi-hard cheese with a propensity to melt into a pool of golden deliciousness. Traditionally made in all alpine areas of Switzerland, it is nonetheless typically associated with the Valais, Switzerland's southern, sun-baked, alpine canton famous for its fighting cows, distinctive wines and great mountain resorts (think Zermatt, Saas Fee and Verbier).

Since the 1960s, when people started getting the raclette habit, production of this cheese has gone into overdrive. The bulk of Swiss-made Raclette cheese ('Raclette Suisse') comes from large dairies dotted around various cantons situated north of the Alps. Made chiefly from pasteurised milk, it does its melting job pretty efficiently but it lacks local character and flavour. For Raclette cheese with real taste and a deeply rooted tradition, you need to get down to the Valais.

In Obergesteln in the serenely beautiful, broad-bottomed Goms valley, Alexander Zenhäusern is employed by a group of local farmers to transform their milk into cheese at the village *Sennerei* (cheese dairy). In summer, the grassy slopes around the village are regularly cut for hay. In between are patchwork strips of potatoes and rye, the only crops that will grow at this altitude. In winter, the valley is cloaked in a thick layer of powder snow. (If you've ever taken the Glacier Express, you've been right through here.)

The origins of Raclette

The name of the cheese is related to *racler*, 'to scrape', a word which evokes the distinctive way in which raclette was traditionally prepared and served in alpine areas. A wheel of cheese was cut in half and the cut surface set at right angles to the fire. As the cut surface melted, it was scraped (*raclé*) onto a plate and served with boiled and cured mountain meats. Nowadays, Swiss cheese shops often lend out special raclette grills at no charge (provided you buy the cheese from them). With this type of grill, which gives a result that most closely approximates raclette melted over an open fire, the cheese is cradled below the grill and heated till the cut surface melts. This is scraped off in the usual way and served with all the trimmings. Commoner still are the small raclette 'ovens' which come complete with little pans. Slices of cheese are laid in the pans and heated till bubbling.

The cheesecloth is readied to scoop up the curds.

Alexander gathers up the curds in cheesecloth with the help of a bendy metal rod, strong arms and teeth.

The drained curds resemble cottage cheese.

When I called Alexander to get the story of his cheese, he seemed puzzled. "There's no story," he responded, "it's just Raclette. Mind you," he added as an afterthought and with a twinkle in his voice, "I've been at it for about 30 years, so I have had a bit of practice – *ich bin ein alter Hase!*" ("I'm an old hare").

Blocks of curd are cut in large squares...

In 1995 when Alexander was hired, seven farmers sent their milk to the dairy. Now there are just four: three of them in Obergesteln and one in Oberwald down the road. "Same volume of milk but fewer farmers," he explains. This trend to consolidate dairy units is reproduced all over the country though Swiss dairy farms remain extremely small by any international standard.

All Alexander's cheeses are made from raw milk. The most celebrated amongst them – the ones that draw a steady stream of local chefs and cheese lovers to the dairy shop – are his Raclette and Gomser cheeses. He also makes Mutschli (see Glossary, page 245), infant cheeses not much bigger than flowerpots and designed to be eaten after only 5–6 weeks' ageing, and Ziger, fresh, ricotta-like whey cheeses which he leaves either in their virginal state, or flavours variously with chives, garlic, curry, parsley, *herbes de Provence* or onion.

...set inside the round moulds...

In summer the milk comes down a pipeline from the alp 800 metres above. "We employ two German women every season to tend the cows," he explains. "Mornings and evenings when they're through with the milking, they give me a call and I open up the valves!" Twenty-five minutes later, the milk is in the dairy.

Cheese making in Alexander's small, tiled dairy follows the usual, comforting rhythm: the raw milk is gently warmed, the starter bacteria and rennet are added

...and pressed to take the shape of the mould.

115

and left till the milk has set. The curds are cut medium-fine, as befits a semi-hard cheese, water is added and the vat is heated some more. Once the curds reach the correct size and consistency, it's time to lift them out of the whey.

With a skill born of 30 years of practice, Alexander gathers up the curds in a capacious square cheesecloth like a mosquito net, using a combination of brawny arms, strong teeth and a bendy metal rod. Then with the help of a pulley suspended over the vat – he works single-handed – he lifts up the mass, swings it away from the vat, squeezes it firmly to extract excess whey and dumps it in the rectangular cheese table, where it is briefly pressed.

Next he divides up the large block of curds into large squares and tosses them into perforated plastic moulds, squashing them firmly in place so they assume the round shape of the mould. After an overnight pressing the infant cheeses will be salted for 24 hours and the ageing process will begin.

Raclette cheese needs at least 4–5 months' maturing for its aromas to develop fully, affirms Alexander. "Cheese is like meat," he says, "it needs to be properly aged." Gomser cheese is aged a little longer – between eight months and a year. It's perfect served in slices with the local air-dried beef and sausages. If the rind is cleaned off and the cheese kept longer still – up to two and a half years – it dries out sufficiently to qualify as Hobelkäse (similar to Berner Hobelkäse, page 49), cut in very thin slices ('*gehobelt*') and rolled up like cannelloni.

In 2007, Raclette cheese made in the Valais gained its AOC designation (see Glossary, page 244). This means that producers in the region who conform to the criteria laid down by the AOC may call their cheese Raclette du Valais AOC. Alexander raises his eyes heavenwards when I ask him if he'd like to apply for AOC status for his cheeses. "What would I want all those officials poking their noses in here for? I've made my cheese the same way for 30 years and people seem to like it well enough," he observes with masterly understatement.

Alexander Zenhäusern
Sennerei Genossenschaft Obergesteln
3988 Obergesteln VS

Tel. 027 973 20 12
info@gomser.ch
www.gomser.ch

Mont Vully

Ewald Schafer is one of Switzerland's new generation of cheese makers. His first tentative moves towards a different model of cheese making came in the early 1990s when he took over the small village dairy in Cressier south of Murten, in the rich farming country of canton Fribourg. At the time, the dairy was making only Emmentaler. For a while Schafer continued to turn out great wheels of the traditional, mild, holey cheese, but his heart wasn't in it. "We're in the permitted production area [for Emmentaler]," he acknowledges, "but this is not its original home – it just didn't feel right." He began to play with the idea of making a semi-hard, medium-sized cheese, packed with flavour – something along the lines of Appenzeller, but special to his dairy.

The following year, in tandem with the Emmentaler production – which Schafer was reluctant to abandon immediately – he started experimenting with his new cheese. He named it Mont Vully, after the renowned vine-covered hillside on the other side of the lake of Murten and whose Pinot Noir is used to wash the rind of his newborn cheese. Mont Vully immediately caught the attention of a handful of cheese-lovers and it looked like it would become a niche product alongside the Emmentaler. But by 1998, Mont Vully had built up such a following that Schafer was able to abandon the big wheels and concentrate solely on his new creation.

In 2003, he added two more Mont Vullys to the range: an organic cheese called Le Bio and an aged cheese with the tag Le Réserve. In 2006, Schafer's efforts were

A wood-panelled house in Cressier.

crowned by an award of best in class at the Swiss Cheese Awards. Mont Vully was established.

Work starts at 7.30 a.m. in this beautiful old wood-fronted dairy (with an apartment upstairs for the Schafer family). The milk is delivered from the farms that Schafer has contracted to supply him. Some of it is organic; all comes from animals that graze outdoors in summer and are fed on hay in winter (silage, which would taint the milk, is outlawed). Because not all the milk is used on the day of delivery (though never stored longer than 48 hours), Schafer chooses to thermise it (see Glossary, page 245), a brief heat treatment which eliminates any potentially undesirable micro-organisms while preserving the good guys that contribute flavour and texture to the cheese. "It's more stable," he affirms, "and it gives me an even result throughout the year."

The milk is then cooled and the starter added, followed by the rennet. The curds are cut and gently heated, then poured into the moulds, perforated to allow the whey to drain off. The newly formed cheeses are pressed with the beautiful

The curds are poured into moulds.

The Mont Vully imprint.

The cheese takes on a burnished colour after brushing with wine.

The colour of the crust deepens further after maturing.

Ewald Schafer carves a generous chunk of
Mont Vully.

Mont Vully imprint of a chubby bunch of
grapes, and remain in their moulds overnight. Next day they are unmoulded and
immersed in brine for 24 hours. As they
mature in the cool, damp cellar below the
dairy, they're turned daily and the crust
brushed with salt water mixed with Pinot
Noir from the Mont Vully vineyards and
annatto colouring.

Mont Vully comes in three strengths:
Classique, aged between 10 and 20 weeks,
has a warm orange crust and a mild but
pleasing flavour. Le Bio, the organic
cheese with a similar ageing profile, is
also mild with a toasty coloured crust
that comes from the addition of lightly
roasted wheat flour. The one with the
most piquant flavour is Le Réserve, whose
crust turns a deep chestnut over the 6–12
months of maturing. You can find Mont
Vully in top cheese shops throughout
Switzerland, at Waitrose in the UK and in
select cheese boutiques in the US.

Ewald Schafer
Fromagerie Schafer
route de l'Ecole 3
1785 Cressier FR

Tel. 026 674 12 37
info@montvullykaese.ch
www.montvullykaese.ch

Bergmatter

Bergmatter is a newly created, semi-hard cheese with an impressively gnarled, chestnut-brown rind, a generous scattering of holes and an incomparably rich flavour. It's one of the cheeses created by Willi Schmid, the celebrated cheese Meister working in Lichtensteig, a small town on the western edge of the rolling, prealpine farmland of Toggenburg, where canton St Gallen bumps up against Appenzell.

Willi was one of eight children growing up on the family dairy farm in the upper Toggenburg. He was fascinated by cheese from an early age, but his training took an unusual, slightly circuitous route. Straight out of school he went to work in different dairies in Switzerland, including a stint at the head of a Sbrinz dairy (see page 60). After some years' practical experience, he signed up at dairy school to study the theory, delved into the science of cheese

making and developed a passionate interest in microbiology, which he refers to affectionately as *Chäferli-Wissenschaft* ('bug science'). Finally, in 2006 he found some tiny premises tucked away down a side street in Lichtensteig and opened up his own business. At the last count Willi made 25 different cheeses, some from cow's, some from goat's and some from sheep's milk. "Surely," I gaped, "you can't have created all 25 in three years?" "As a matter of fact," he said, giving me a sideways grin, "it took me just a month! I had all these ideas running around in my head and I just had to try them out." He decided to start out making small quantities, and see how things went. The plan was to focus on the ones that sold and forget the rest. In the event they all found a ready market. Five years on he's still making them all, and trying to keep abreast of demand.

A selection of Willi Schmid's cheeses, clockwise from top left: Jersey Blue, Bergmatter, Caprinello, Vivienne, Jersey Blue and Bergfichte.

Willi Schmid gives a Bergmatter cheese its daily brushing with brine.

Of all the cheeses Willi makes, I sense he has a distinctly soft spot for his Bergmatter. He describes it as a cheese *'für Liebhaber'*, reserved for real enthusiasts – just as well, as production is tiny, and limited to the winter months between November and April. The milk for Bergmatter, from a small local herd of Brown Swiss cows, is delivered in the morning and gently heated to prepare it to receive three different starter cultures. Amongst them is one which Willi selects for the "sweetish aromas" that it brings to the finished cheese. For cow's milk cheese like this one, Willi uses calves' rennet; for goat's milk cheeses, kid's rennet and for sheep's milk cheese lamb's rennet.

"You don't really need to match the rennet to the cheese," he explains, "but I like to – it feels right."

Once set, the curd is heated and cut in small grains and water is added, typically for semi-hard cheese. When the cheeses are formed, the wheels are pressed for about an hour and a half before being plunged into the *Salzbad* (brine). Finally they go into the cellar to embark on their eight-month ripening process. During this time, the wheels are faithfully turned and brushed with brine, which draws out more whey, builds up the chestnut-brown rind and helps to develop the rich flavour.

With its deep brown, wonky, wrinkly rind, Bergmatter looks every inch the cheese for real enthusiasts: no mechanised process could ever produce something so delightfully anarchical, so utterly unique. The gnarled rind conceals a smooth interior, buttery yellow with a rash of pea-sized holes. The smell takes you straight up into the hayloft, with gentle wafts of manure thrown in. In the mouth it's smooth, gently yielding, with unfolding layers of rich, buttery, long-lasting flavour. If you're lucky enough to live within reach of Willi's Städtlichäsi in Lichtensteig, you can buy (or order) Bergmatter direct; Globus, Manor and some specialist stores also stock it, and tiny quantities are exported.

Willi Schmid
Städtlichäsi Lichtensteig
Farbgasse 3
9620 Lichtensteig

Tel. 071 994 32 86
mail@willischmid.com
www.willischmid.com

MORE SEMI-HARD CHEESES

Aletsch Grand Cru
Urs Bützberger
Käserei Aletsch-Goms
3982 Bitsch VS

Andeerer Via Spluga
Martin Bienerth
Sennerei Andeer
7440 Andeer GR

Andeerer Traum u. Gourmet
Martin Bienerth
Sennerei Andeer
7440 Andeer GR

Eolienne
Fromagerie Spielhofer
2610 St-Imier BE

Entlebucher Bärgblüemli-Chäs
Franz Renggli
Bergkäserei Oberberg
6170 Schüpfheim LU

Erguel
Fromagerie Spielhofer
2610 St-Imier BE

Le Fortin
Michel Beroud
Fromagerie Fleurette
1659 Rougemont VD

Galmizer
Walter Haussener
Käserei
3285 Galmiz FR

Gstaader Bergkäse
Erhard Kohli
3780 Gstaad BE

Major Benoît
Didier Germain
Fromagerie Les Martel
2316 Les Ponts-de-Martel NE

Milchmännerchäs
Marcel Tobler Käserei
9414 Schachen b. Reute AR

Mont Soleil
Fromagerie Spielhofer
2610 St-Imier BE

Mühlestein
Willi Schmid
Städtlichäsi
9620 Lichtensteig SG

Obwalder Bratkäse
Felix Schibli
Seiler Käserei AG
6060 Sarnen OW

Passo dello Spluga
Jürg Flükiger
Sennerei Genossenschaft
7435 Splügen GR

Sörenberger Bergkäse
Franz Troxler
Entlebucher Spezialitäten Käserei AG
6170 Schüpfheim LU

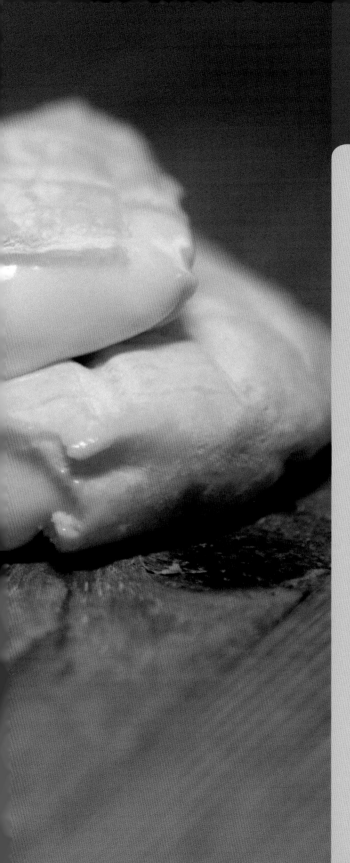

SOFT CHEESES

The cheeses in this chapter include two kinds: the washed-rind variety with a pinkish-orange crust; and the bloomy-rind variety with a snowy-white rind, like the bloom on a freshly picked plum or grape (hence the name).

The process for making these two is different from that followed for hard and semi-hard cheeses in earlier chapters. The milk is barely heated and the curds gently cut in large pieces. They are not pressed but tipped into moulds and left to drain beneath their own weight. The cheeses are then briefly salted and aged for anything from a few days to some weeks. During their *affinage* (maturing) both washed-rind and bloomy-rind varieties are regularly turned to ensure even ripening. Washed-rind cheeses get special treatment with a salt solution or some kind of aromatic mixture. Both have a high moisture content and a correspondingly short shelf life.

These are speciality cheeses, which make superb contributions to the cheese board, either served solo and unadorned, or in combination with hard and semi-hard varieties.

•

Vacherin Mont d'Or AOC

I n a world where everything we eat seems to be available all year round and where our food is increasingly an anonymous commodity undistinguished by links to either place or season, Vacherin Mont d'Or stands out a mile. This small, washed-rind cheese bound by a band of spruce bark is one of those rare, strictly local, seasonal delights that still punctuate the Swiss cheese calendar. It's made only between 15 August and 31 March in and around the Vallée de Joux in the Jura mountains of canton Vaud.

When the days shorten and winter looms, treat yourself to a Vacherin

A wintry landscape in the Vallée de Joux, home of Vacherin Mont d'Or.

The curds and whey are poured into the moulds.

Note how large the curds arte cut.

Mont d'Or. Lift the lid from the box and let the cheese come to room temperature for an hour or two. Then dig in, take a piece into your mouth and roll it slowly, tentatively, over your tongue. Close your eyes and allow yourself to be transported up into the Jura.

The night-time temperatures are beginning to dip below zero, the mountain air is crisp and sweet, the manicured hill farm pastures, grazed in summer by speckled brown cows, are white now with the first dusting of snow. In the little village of Le Lieu (400 inhabitants) on the Lac de Joux, Monsieur Hauser is hard at work on his Vacherin Mont d'Or. He's one of only around 20 producers left in the area (30 years ago there were three times that number), and he's intensely proud of his cheese. From September to March he makes Vacherin Mont d'Or. The rest of the year he makes Gruyère – the typical pat-

tern for cheese makers in the Joux Valley.

The small village dairy is warm and humid, full of soothing, bovine smells. The milk for this semi-soft, washed-rind cheese, must first be thermised (see boxed text page 133 and Glossary page 245) and cooled before cheese making can begin. The starter, which will give the Vacherin its inimitable flavour and character, is stirred into the vat, followed at a decent interval by a dose of rennet. Once the milk is set, the comb-like cheese harp is drawn briefly back and forth to cut the curds in walnut-sized blobs. These are scooped into big white buckets and tipped into tall, perforated plastic cylinders set on draining tables.

In another corner of the dairy the fragrant strips of mahogany-coloured spruce bark that will embrace the infant cheeses are softened up in boiling water. They perfume the air like a herb-infused

A Vacherin Mont d'Or ready for market.

The finished cheeses are coaxed into their boxes.

The spruce bands are steamed till soft.

Cylindrical moulds filled with steaming curds.

sauna. All around is an impressive panoply of buckets, brushes, soap squirters, disinfectant baths, high-pressure hoses and gallons upon gallons of water, all of them prerequisites for the scrupulous hygiene required when working with milk and cheese products, particularly where soft cheeses are concerned.

The fresh curds, set firm by their own weight, are unmoulded from their perforated plastic cylinders, somehow miraculously holding their shape. Monsieur Hauser slices them horizontally and tosses the slices nonchalantly across the stainless steel surface. There they are retrieved by another pair of hands and each cheese is braced by the spruce strips. An elastic band is snapped around to hold the spruce in place during the cheese's ripening period – 17 to 25 days in the cool, damp cellar next door.

The final task of the morning for Hauser's small team of helpers is to box

The freshly formed cheeses are sliced...

...wrapped in spruce bands...

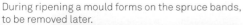

During ripening a mould forms on the spruce bands, to be removed later.

...and set on wooden shelves to ripen.

up a batch of perfectly mature cheeses ready for market. The pale wooden boxes stamped with the dairy's name are made purposely slightly smaller than the finished product, so that when the cheeses are deftly coaxed into their containers, the pinkish-gold crust erupts into a sort of ecstatic, voluptuous wave.

In this corner of the Jura, both the Swiss and their French neighbours across the border make a version of Vacherin. The Swiss cheese's full title is Vacherin Mont d'Or, while the French cheese calls itself simply Mont d'Or or Vacherin du Haut Doubs. Both kinds are protected by an AOC (see Glossary page 244) which means they're made only in a strictly circum-

scribed area and subject to certain precise conditions. The AOC regulations for the French cheeses stipulate raw milk. Since 1985 the Swiss cheeses have been made from thermised milk. The French cheeses have a slightly more forward flavour and pale beige crust; the Swiss cheeses are a little milder with a pinkish rind. Both, when ripened to perfection, have a delectably runny consistency. The spruce bark gives a gentle but not overly pungent aroma, the flesh is luscious and silky, like heavy cream that's come of age.

The presentation of Vacherin Mont d'Or is distinctive – the cheese is always sold in its spruce wood box, whose weight is part of the price.

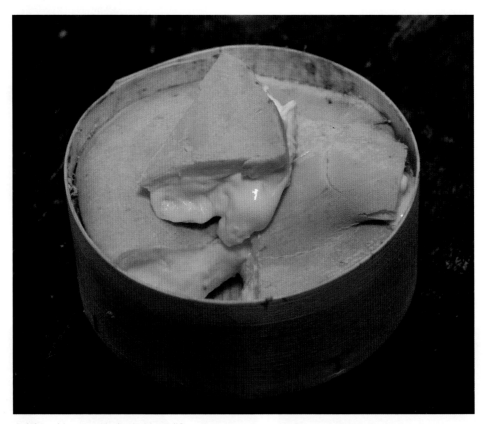

A delectably runny Vacherin Mont d'Or.

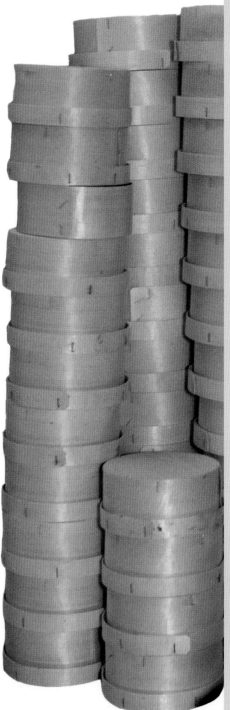

Vacherin Mont d'Or, raw milk and thermised milk

In the 1980s Swiss Vacherin Mont d'Or was blighted by a series of listeriosis outbreaks. Most people are under the impression that these occurred in cheeses made from raw milk. "People assume that we started thermising milk as a result of listeriosis," observes Jean-Michel Rochat, an *affineur* (cheese ripener) at Les Charbonnières on the Lac de Joux. "Actually we started in 1985, two years before the worst outbreak. We'd been having problems since the 1970s and we were convinced thermisation was the solution." In fact thermisation solved nothing; if anything it lulled the cheese makers into a false sense of security.

The problem, it is now acknowledged, was not in the milk, but in the dairy and the ripening cellars (so-called 'post-process contamination'). In tests performed following the 1987 outbreak, a batch of perfectly healthy milk was made into cheese outside the area, then transported to 12 cellars where Vacherin Mont d'Or had always been made. The cheese was ripened, as ever, on wooden boards, and brushed daily with salt water. After three weeks the cheese was tested and found to contain *Listeria monocytogenes*, the bacteria which causes listeriosis. Cheese production was shut down for some months, all the dairies were rigorously cleaned, disinfected and re-equipped to new, rigorous standards. Slowly, production resumed, though it has never regained its former volume. The listeriosis tragedy is now a distant, though still painful, memory. Vacherin Mont d'Or is once again a superb and wholly safe product to eat.

Why the box? The reason is obvious once you plunge in. If the cheese were not firmly corseted in this way, it would quite simply run away with the spoon. Attempts to release it from its corset or to broach it with anything other than a spoon will certainly end in tears, for inside it's nothing but a pool of molten gold. Serve this delectably runny cheese with good rye or wholewheat bread, or allow it to slither gently over small, waxy (or new) potatoes cooked in their skins. Serve also a selection of fragrant, smoked meats and mountain sausages.

Another option is to bake Vacherin Mont d'Or in the oven, for a sort of mini-fondue: take a sheet of aluminium foil and place a box of Vacherin Mont d'Or on top. Remove the lid and gather up the foil around the edge of the box to prevent any leakage, but don't cover the cheese. Pierce the top with a fork in several places, make a few incisions in the cheese with a sharp knife and insert some slivers of garlic, if wished. You can also dribble in a little white wine, though this may be gilding the lily. Heat the oven to 200°C and bake the cheese in its box for about 25 minutes or until melted. Serve cubes of crusty bread or small waxy potatoes (or new potatoes) for dipping in, plus a selection of pickles and cured and smoked meats on the side.

Fromagerie Hauser
Les Terreaux 8
1345 Le Lieu VD

....

Tel. 021 841 11 40
www.vacherin-montdor.ch/
fr/affineurs.htm

Charles Hauser proud
shows a pair of cheese

Fleurette –
Tomme de vache au lait cru

Swiss Tommes – generically speaking – are small, soft, bloomy-rind cheeses (think Camembert) made generally of cow's milk, sometimes goat's milk, and occasionally a combination of the two. Quite different in texture, taste and size from French Tommes (which are medium-sized and generally semi-hard, as Tomme de Savoie), they've been made since at least the nineteenth century, often on a domestic scale and designed to be eaten when just a few days old. Sometimes they were the soft siblings of bigger, harder cheeses with which they shared the dairy, made from small quantities of milk left over after the big cheese had had its turn.

Nowadays, most Swiss-made Tommes are produced on an industrial scale from pasteurised milk. They have a thickish downy rind, soapy texture and little flavour. There is one Swiss Tomme that stands out from the crowd. Developed in the 1990s by *fromager* Michel Beroud in the small village dairy of Rougemont in the Pays d'Enhaut of canton Vaud, it's called Fleurette, subtitled Tomme de vache au lait cru. As the name indicates, it's made from raw milk. Matured just long enough (between eight and ten days) to develop a mind of its own, Fleurette runs about in a deliciously undisciplined sort of way. It tastes sublime, with layers of rich, creamy flavour that unfold on the tongue and persist long after the cheese has been swallowed. *"C'est bon ça, putain que c'est bon!"*, exclaimed the famous French food writer and broadcaster Jean-Pierre Coffe when offered a taste, *"un vrai fromage qui sent la ferme!"* ("Jeez, that's good! A real cheese that tastes and smells of the farm!")

It's often supposed that Fleurette was a Beroud creation. In fact the Rougemont dairy was producing it, albeit on a small scale, before Michel arrived on the scene. What has changed is the quantity made: when he took over as cheese maker in 1989, the dairy was transforming 30,000 litres of milk into cheese each year; nowadays, the figure hovers around 650,000 litres annually – which gives an idea of how successful this gifted cheese maker has been. Today, other specialities have joined Fleurette, all of them from raw milk. There's a larger bloomy-rind one called Le Délice, a washed-rind soft cheese known as Le Rubloz, a semi-hard called Le Fortin and a hard cheese which he's named Fromage des Forts. But it's the saucer-sized, bloomy-rind Fleurette which has become the Rougemont dairy's signature cheese.

The breakthrough came when internationally renowned chef Frédy Girardet (who has a chalet in nearby Schönried) discovered Fleurette. "It was a bit of luck to have him as a customer," admits the cheese maker. "He was very critical, but

A contented cow grazes in a wild flower meadow.

combining the chilled evening milk with the morning milk. "I can still remember when they used to pull in the churns on sledges on freezing cold winter mornings," smiles Michel.

The starter bacteria, a batch of whey reserved from yesterday's cheese making, is added first. Then the milk is heated to barely lukewarm and the rennet stirred in. Once the milk has set, the curds are broken up into large, walnut-sized globs, pumped from the vat into small, cylindrical, perforated moulds and left to drain, pressed only by their own weight.

"How long will they drain?" I ask. "Ah," responds Beroud with a smile, "we're working with raw milk here – *c'est pas moi qui décide – c'est le lait!*" ("it's not me who decides: it's the milk!") He touches briefly on the various factors that can affect the cheese-making process and influence the speed at which things progress, ranging from the temperature both outside and inside the dairy, the cows' rations (grass in summer, hay in winter), and where they are in their lactation cycle.

Once the cheeses are formed, the perforated cylinders are lifted off to reveal

fair – at the beginning he sent some back and told me that improvements were needed. It was tough," he adds, "but it was a big help."

In March 2000, at Michel's instigation, a state-of-the-art *fromagerie* was built at the entrance to the village, just opposite the sixteenth-century château and the fine old Romanesque church which shelters under its huge sloping roof. The dairy building is designed to meet the latest EU specifications and big enough to enable a slight increase in production ("not too much – we want to remain artisanal"). It's owned by a cooperative of milk producers who farm in and around the village; Michel is their tenant. He contracts to buy their milk, for which he pays above the market rate. All the animals are pastured in summer and fed on hay in winter. No silage is allowed in the feed. "It's their [the farmers'] *fromagerie*" he adds, "so it's in their interests to supply me with good milk so I can make a good product." The farmers deliver once a day in the morning,

Rougemont's Romanesque church and adjoining château, just opposite Michel Beroud's dairy.

Freshly formed Fleurette cheeses.

Cheeses are laid on wire racks and salted.

Michel Beroud inspects a batch of Fleurettes.

little white discs of infant cheese. These are laid on wire racks, sprinkled with salt and then transferred on their racks to a cool, damp cellar. Within a few days a downy duvet of white mould starts to form on the surface – *"la croûte commence à fleurir"* ("the rind begins to bloom") is how Michel describes it.

After between six and ten days' ripening the cheeses are ready to roll. Michel invites us down to the cellar to inspect the finished Fleurettes. Amongst the serried ranks of bloomy white cheeses, we can't help noticing, to our consternation, that a whole batch seems to be covered in little black specks. With a perfectly straight face, Michel explains that "those ones fell on the floor," hastening to assure us that "they'll be fine once we've cleaned them up a bit." Then we notice his moustache twitching imperceptibly, and he bursts into helpless chuckles, visibly delighted at the joke. "As a matter of fact," he confesses, wiping his eyes, "it's a small batch that's rolled in chopped truf-

fles – I made them specially for the hotels in Gstaad for the Christmas period!"

In the final step the Fleurettes – with or without truffles – are hand-wrapped in the *fromagerie's* distinctive white and blue waxed paper. Then there's a brief, three-week window in which to savour this wonderful cheese at its most fragrant.

You can find Fleurettes in specialist shops throughout Switzerland. Beroud is selective about which ones to sell to – "raw milk cheese is a living product, it's constantly on the move," he stresses, "we need to be sure there are people who know how to store the cheeses properly and keep an eye on them as they mature." Fleurette also finds its way onto the cheese trolleys of Switzerland's top restaurants and tiny quantities are exported.

Fleurette ready to roll.

Michel Beroud
Fromagerie Fleurette
1659 Rougemont VD

Tel. 026 925 82 10
michel-beroud@bluewin.ch
www.tommefleurette.ch

Switzerland: champion of raw milk cheeses

In most industrialised countries, pasteurised cheese is the norm, raw milk cheese the exception. Switzerland is different. Here, though some cheese is made from thermised or pasteurised milk (see Glossary page 245) the great majority of cheese is made from fresh, healthy, raw milk. One reason is that the Swiss overwhelmingly make large, hard cheeses whose acidity, salt content, lack of moisture and long ageing create an environment where unwelcome bacteria cannot thrive. Another is that cheese making remains a small-scale, local operation with milk sourced from the cheese makers' own animals or from farms close to the dairy.

That cheese seeths with bacteria is an undeniable – for some, alarming – fact. But as Piero Sardo of Slow Food's Foundation for Biodiversity points out, there are good microbes and bad microbes, and the vast majority of bacteria found in raw milk are benign. They enable the cheese-making process to happen. It's harder to make cheese from pasteurised milk because most of the helpful bacteria have been eliminated), and they contribute local character and extra dimensions of flavour.

Food scientist Harold McGee explains (in *On Food and Cooking*) that "raw milk sours into wholesome foods because the acid-producing bacteria have certain advantages, including a head start, over less helpful microbes. Pasteurised milk...is nearly free of bacteria, and troublemakers have a better chance of prevailing." This is why almost all cheese-related food scares involve pasteurised cheeses. Raw milk cheese that's properly handled and carefully monitored, as is the case in Switzerland, is a safe, natural, tasty choice.

141

Stanser Fladä

Sepp Barmettler is one of the new generation whose cheeses first set noses twitching and tastebuds tickling in the early 1990s. Sepp's father had founded the Barmettler dairy business in 1960 in Stans, a grand little town at the foot of the Stanserhorn mountain and minutes from Lake Lucerne. Their speciality was Bratchäs, the classic semi-hard melting cheese (similar to Raclette) that's typical of central Switzerland. Sepp began to toy with the idea of doing something different; he just wasn't yet quite sure what.

Stans is in the heart of Sbrinz country, so one option might have been to add this huge, extra-hard cheese to the Barmettler Bratchäs offering. In those days, recalls Sepp, all cheese making was centrally regulated – as regards both type and quantity – by the Swiss Cheese Union. He duly applied to make Sbrinz, but permission was refused on the basis that the Barmettler dairy was too small. "So I decided to experiment instead with some new cheeses" says the lean, bespectacled, white-coated Sepp, who looks more like a scientist than a working cheese maker. A potential setback was thus converted into an opportunity – for the cheese maker, whose creative instincts were given full rein, and for cheese-lovers both at home and abroad.

The dairy still makes Bratchäs, a favourite amongst local customers for their raclette feasts. But it's the newer cheeses that have established Sepp's reputation as a maker of 'Käse der Extraklasse' – seriously classy cheeses, as his brochure and cheese-wrapping paper proudly proclaim. First came a Mutschli-type cheese

(see Glossary page 244) called Stanserhornchäsli, created to celebrate the centenary of the Stanserhorn cable car, which rises from the town centre. To this have now been added Stanser Röteli, a toothsome, semi-soft Reblochon-type cheese and – the standout for me – Stanser Fladä, a washed-rind cheese with a pinkish, crumpled crust and a wickedly oozy interior. Later still Sepp embarked on some sheep's milk cheeses (see page 174).

From a cautious start making just 1000 kilos of Fladä per year, Sepp progressed steadily to the current annual level of around 20,000 kilos. He makes the cheese two or three times a week, each batch yielding 380 of these stinky little treasures.

The raw material comes from around a dozen dairy farmers in the neighbourhood. Even now, with Sepp's cheeses well and truly launched, at least two-thirds of the milk goes to make non-cheese milk specialities (yogurt, quark, etc.) – "I couldn't live by my cheese alone," admits Sepp honestly, "there's just not enough volume."

While the milk is resolutely local, all the starter cultures come from specialist laboratories in France, renewed with each

Sepp cuts the curds in large pieces...

...and tips the curds into perforated moulds.

successive batch of cheese. "I make several different cheeses" he explains, "and I don't make cheese every day, so I can't keep back some starter each time to add to the next batch, as cheese makers do who are working daily with big volumes of milk and a single variety of cheese."

Once set, the cultured and renneted milk is warmed to barely blood heat, cut into walnut-sized pieces and stirred. For a soft, washed-rind cheese like Fladä, the curds must be treated with infinite tenderness, barely heated, scarcely cut, and gently stirred. This way only the smallest amount of whey is released, maximum moisture is retained and the resulting cheese is damp and delectable.

After about half an hour of gentle heating and stirring, the curds are tipped carefully into moulds and left to drain, pressed only by their own weight. Once firm, the cheeses are slipped out of their moulds, brined and set on shelves in Sepp's cool, damp cellar. Now the all-important maturing process begins. Over

the next two to four weeks the cheeses will be brushed with a salt solution and turned three times a week so that maturing proceeds evenly and the cheeses don't stick to the wooden boards. Encouraged by these gentle ministrations, the pinkish rind begins to form and the cheese ripens to runny perfection. To serve the delectable Fladä, instructs Sepp, slice away the top and scoop out the silky, molten flesh with a spoon. Serve it with good country-style or sourdough bread or small new potatoes cooked in their skins.

You can find Fladä (and other Barmettler delicacies) at the dairy shop on Stans's Dorfplatz, or you can order cheese online from the dairy for delivery within Switzerland. Sepp's specialities also find their way onto the cheese boards of top restaurants like Jasper in Luzerne's Palace Hotel. Small quantities can even be found in high-end outlets abroad such as Artisanal, New York's famous speciality cheese store.

The curd for soft cheeses is cut much larger than for hard.

The cylinders filled to the brim with curds.

Pressed under their own weight, they compact and reduce in size.

Fishing out stray pieces of curd from the bottom of the vat.

Josef Barmettler
Barmettler Molkerei AG
Dorfplatz 9
6370 Stans NW

Tel. 041 619 09 95
www.cheesenet.ch
jb@cheesenet.ch

p. 146/147→
A typically romanticised nineteenth-century view of Lake Lucerne painted by a well-known English painter William Collingwood Smith.

Bergfichte

The name of this soft, washed-
rind cheese from Willi Schmid in
Lichtensteig (see page 122) gives
a clue to its special character: braced by
a strip of spruce bark (*Fichte*), it's powerfully redolent of the mountains (*Bergen*).
With just a whiff of its pinkish smeared
rind and surrounding spruce band and a
taste of its sinfully creamy flesh, you'll be
instantly transported up into the prealpine Toggenburg hills dotted with tall
Norway spruces, their branches bent
under the weight of freshly fallen snow.

The milk for Bergfichte, from a local
herd of Brown Swiss cows, is delivered
daily throughout the year to the back
door of the Städtlichäsi, Willi's small
town dairy. To make a cheese of this type,

the milk requires gentle heating so as to
conserve all its wonderful aromas, and re-
spectful treatment as the cheese is coaxed
to maturity. First the warmed curds are
cut in walnut-sized pieces and carefully
transferred into tall, cylindrical plastic
moulds. After about an hour, much of the
whey has leaked through the perforated
sides of the moulds and the cheeses are
firm enough to hold their shape. They are
encircled with a supple band of spruce
bark, which braces the cheese and gives it
a tannic, slightly resinous flavour.

Finally the cheeses take a one-hour
dip in brine, after which they're stacked
on racks to dry out for a bit and then laid
on spruce boards in the cellar to complete the ripening. For six to eight weeks

Milk churns by the back door of Willi Schmid's dairy.

the little wheels are turned and brushed ('smeared') daily with salt water. Gradually the rind deepens in colour from its initial ivory to a peachy-orange and the flavour advances from mild to deliciously mature.

Bergfichte is the kind of cheese that should play a starring – perhaps even solo – role at the cheese course. Slice away

the pinkish upper crust, dig into the flesh with a spoon, close your eyes and treasure the taste. In texture and in flavour, it's a kind of cross between Vacherin Mont d'Or and Reblochon, unbelievably succulent and creamy with a real taste of the mountains.

Willi Schmid
Städtlichäsi Lichtensteig
Farbgasse 3
9620 Lichtensteig SG

Tel. 071 994 32 86
mail@willischmid.com
www.willischmid.com

MORE SOFT CHEESES

Le Délice
Michel Beroud
Fromagerie Fleurette
1659 Rougemont VD

Senne-Flade
Paul Bieri Käserei
8340 Hinwil ZH

Petit Jura
Florilait SA
Courtemelon
2852 Courtételle JU

Tomme vaudoise
Jean-Daniel Perren
1608 Chesalles-sur-Oron VD

Rose d'Ogoz
Nicolas Charrière
1608 Vuisternens-en-Ogoz FR

Weichkäse mit Weissschimmel
Fritz Gerber
6197 Schangnau BE

Le Rubloz
Michel Beroud
Fromagerie Fleurette
1659 Rougemont VD

Weichling
Markus Stirnimann
6156 Luthern LU

Willi holds Jersey Blue in his right hand, Bergfichte and Vivienne in his left. In front of him is a Caprinello.

p. 152/153 →
A devout family with pets praying before their cheese supper.

Goat's and Sheep's Milk Cheeses

Goats and sheep predated cattle in the Alps and have always been a feature of the Swiss landscape – at least four major goat breeds, Alpine, Toggenburg, Oberhasli and Saanen, originated here. So it's surprising that Switzerland – unlike France – never developed a strong tradition of cheese made from their milk. This is changing fast, however, and in recent years production and consumption of both goat's and sheep's milk cheeses have grown exponentially in Switzerland. From the producers' angle, there are a number of attractions. Setting up a goat or sheep unit is infinitely less complicated and expensive than establishing a dairy farm; and both goat's and sheep's milk command a higher price than cow's milk. Add to this the fact that 40 per cent of Swiss farms are in mountainous regions, ideally suited to these hardy, nimble animals, and the appeal for Switzerland's farmers becomes even more obvious.

From the consumer's point of view, too, there are plenty of pluses. Many people perceive goat or sheep farming as somehow more 'natural' than dairying: herds are smaller and the agricultural model by its nature less intensive. Also, as more and more people seem to have trouble tolerating cow's milk products, the better digestibility of both goat's and sheep's milk works in their favour. Finally, the Swiss, raised on cow's milk cheeses, are getting more adventurous and are willing to try out cheeses made from these speciality milks with their often more robust flavours. In canton Fribourg, home of both Gruyère AOC and Vacherin Fribourgeois AOC and the almost sacrosanct *moitié-moitié* fondue that combines these two, cheese maker François Jaquet (page 166) has pioneered a fondue mix which is a runaway success – made entirely of goat's cheese.

•

Eighteenth-century goatherds serenade their goats.

Tommes de Chèvre and Chèvre mi-sec

High above Montreux with its five-star hotels, dizzying views out over Lake Geneva and sleekly groomed vineyards, is the little village of Glion. It's a surprising place to find goats. Serge Lenoir and his wife Claude-Lise, came up here in 1980 in search of a more natural, simple lifestyle. They found a rustic smallholding on the edge of the forest above the village. Here they installed themselves and raised three boys.

After about 15 years they started cautiously with a few goats, making a little cheese for their own consumption and to sell locally. These days Serge has around 50 animals, the black-faced, caramel-coated Oberhasli or *chamoisée* breed. Together with Claude-Lise, he makes three different kinds of cheese, all from raw milk: a range of soft, fresh ones variously flavoured and ready within three days of fabrication; a *mi-sec* (semi-dry) – like a French *crottin* – best after about ten days; and a semi-hard, lightly cooked, pressed cheese, which Serge ages for two months.

The Lenoirs follow the goats' natural rhythms, which means cheese is made only between March and November. During the winter months the farm becomes a maternity unit: after coming on heat in September, the goats get pregnant and give birth five months later. When the kids are born in spring, the males are sold for their meat, which is why you find kid (*Gitzi* or *cabri*) on sale in specialist butchers' shops around Easter time. The females are kept on to assure the future of the herd. The cycle then resumes with twice-daily milking and once-a-day cheese making from spring to year's end.

The curd from goat's milk takes longer to set than cow's milk, explained Claude-Lise, so it suits her to spread out the cheese-making procedure over three days. The day I visited – a Friday – Claude-Lise was working with the combined milk from Wednesday evening and Thursday morning, soured and thickened by the culture and rennet and left to stand until that morning. She ladled out the thickly set curds from a stainless steel pail. The curds destined for the *mi-sec* cheeses were ladled into a cheesecloth-lined, bottomless ring to allow more whey to drain off and give a slightly drier result. The remaining curd, for the moister fresh cheeses, was scooped directly into small, straight-sided, perforated plastic cups.

Both kinds were then left to drain on a rack set over a gleaming stainless steel draining board. The following day the plump little white discs would be sprinkled with table salt, turned and left for another 24 hours.

resh goat's cheeses from and Claude-Lise Lenoir.

A curious goat keeps an eye on things.

Some of the soft cheeses are dunked in crushed peppercorns, or chopped chives, or caraway seeds; others are left *nature*. The *mi-sec* cheeses are matured for ten days, during which time they develop a slightly crinkled rind. All the cheeses are wrapped, finally, in clear film stamped with the Lenoirs' name and address and a line drawing of a skipping goat.

Freshly salted goat's cheeses.

The Lenoirs sell their cheeses at Vevey's lively Saturday morning market down by the lake, and in several specialist *fromageries* in the region as well as at the farm. Local restaurants are faithful customers too, from the warm and welcoming Le Jaman in the village to the elegant Michelin-starred L'Ermitage down on Montreux's lakeside. "We're well placed here – there's lots of interest in local products, and a real appreciation for what we're doing," comments Serge.

Serge Lenoir
route des Avants 22
1823 Glion VD

021 963 61 50

Fresh goat's cheese
with crushed peppe
and caraway seed

La chevrette

FROMAGE DE CHEVRE AU LAIT CRU

MG 45%

CH 5996

Fabricant - Affineur
**Michel Beroud
1659 Rougemont**

Pays- d'Enhaut

La Chevrette

When Michel Beroud (see page 136) started making this soft, bloomy-rind goat's cheese, it was a trip down memory lane for him. There were always a few goats on the family farm in Ecoteaux in canton Vaud where he grew up. One day, when Beroud was about 12 years old, his father suggested he might like to make some cheese with the goat's milk. He played around, experimenting with setting the milk and shaping soft fresh cheeses in little cups. "It was like a game," he recalls with a delighted twinkle in his eye, "I used to take them round to the local shop on my bike – and they bought them!"

A few years ago, the teenage son of one of the farmers in Rougemont came round to Beroud's dairy with a couple of litres of his own goat's milk. "Would you like to buy it?" asked the young man, eagerly. "It was like turning the clock back – how could I resist?" grins Beroud. With the milk he made a few fresh Tommes de Chèvre. "It got me thinking – I wanted to give this young chap the possibility of doing something of his own, just like I did, to earn a bit of pocket money."

From there the whole thing snowballed. Some of Beroud's cow's milk suppliers also keep goats, so Beroud asked them to swell the small quantities supplied by the teenager. Then he began to experiment with a soft, bloomy-rind cheese along the lines of his now famous Fleurette. La Chevrette was born.

The procedure is the same as for Fleurette, but the quantities are much smaller and Chevrettes are made only on Mondays and Thursdays. After between seven and nine days' ageing, they're good to go. And because Beroud uses the same bloomy-rind starter bacteria as for his Fleurette, these little cheeses ripen and run about in just the same agreeable way. The flavour is distinctive, but only gently goaty. Try Chevrette with rye bread or seed-speckled biscuits, or small waxy potatoes cooked in their skins.

Michel Beroud
Fromagerie Fleurette
1659 Rougemont VD

Tel. 026 925 82 10
michel-beroud@bluewin.ch
www.tommefleurette.ch

165

Le Vieux Chevrier

Most goat's cheese in Switzerland is of the soft, fresh variety; a handful are semi-soft, like Michel Beroud's Chevrette (page 165). In another category altogether are the much larger, semi-hard goat's cheeses, similar in size and style to Raclette or Vacherin Fribourgeois. One of these, named Le Vieux Chevrier or the Old Goatherd, is made by François Jaquet, who lives and works in the historic village of Grandvillard in the picturesque Intyamon Valley in canton Fribourg.

This is cow country, the cradle of Gruyère AOC and Vacherin Fribourgeois AOC. Goats are less common, though they're growing in popularity. Jaquet had always made cow's milk cheese (mainly Vacherin Fribourgeois) but in 2000 he began to keep goats. Now with a herd of 80 *chamoisées*, the brown-coated, black-faced breed, plus some milk which he buys in, his goat's cheese production has overtaken his cows' milk cheeses. The goats graze close to the farm all summer; in winter when the valley is covered in snow, they're kept indoors. For 300 days a year they're milked twice a day. The remaining three months they're on maternity leave. "It gives me a bit of a break," smiles François.

Making goat's cheese was an entirely new departure for him, and the experience

Shelves stacked with *Vieux Chevrier*.

quite different from working with cow's milk. "Goat's milk varies a lot from one week to another, one season to another. You just keep learning, you don't count the hours – or the cheeses thrown away. You need to be passionate about what you're doing," he adds.

Besides Le Vieux Chevrier, Jaquet makes some soft fresh goat's cheeses and a bloomy-rind, greyish-brown, square cheese called Le Pavé ('paving stone'), which he ages for three weeks. His *tout-chèvre* ('all-goat') fondue mix, La Cabriolle, made of a mixture of semi-hard cheeses of differ-

ing ripeness and sold vacuum-packed in selected outlets (but not supermarkets) all over French-speaking Switzerland, has been a runaway success. But the star of the show is undoubtedly Le Vieux Chevrier. Aged about two and half months, the flesh is pale straw-yellow, with recognisable but not overly assertive goat flavours and a smooth, melt-in-the-mouth texture. To Jaquet's delight, the cheese earned him a gold medal at the 2009 Mountain Cheese Olympics. "You don't get rich winning medals," he grins, *"mais ça motive!"* (but it's motivating).

François Jaquet
La Cabriolle SA
1666 Grandvillard FR
....
Tel. 079 341 80 77
www.lacabriolle.ch
jaquet@lacabriolle.ch

Schafnidelchäsli

When Andreas Gauch studied at the Landwirtschaftss-chule (agricultural school) in Muri in canton Aargau in the 1980s, his interest in sheep farming raised a few eyebrows. Switzerland is a dairy country and the school curriculum was unapologetically cow-centred. "Sheep's milk products were unheard of then," he recalls, "but I wanted to do something different." His studies completed, Andreas returned to the fold, converted his father's farm to organic and bought seven ewes. First he made yogurt, then butter, ice cream and quark, a fresh soft cheese like *fromage frais*. Finally came his now celebrated soft, bloomy-rind sheep's milk cheese called Schafnidelchäsli – which translates roughly as 'creamy little sheep's milk cheese'.

On a crisp winter's morning, Andreas's 50, floppy-eared, hornless Lacaune ewes (the same breed whose milk is used to make Roquefort) were huddled close together for warmth in their large barn. The ram was recognisable by (among other things) the bell around his neck. "It's not for the ewes' benefit," he explained, "it's for mine – I like to know exactly where he is!" Rams can be pretty rough and are quite capable of tackling and bringing down unwary entrants to the field or pen. Broken legs are not uncommon.

Twice a week Andreas makes a batch of his little Schafnidelchäsli. They're small (100g each) and dumpy, like a French *Crottin goat's* cheese in size and appearance. When he started cheese making in 2000, Andreas used raw milk.

Two years ago the regulations governing raw milk cheeses, always subject to severe scrutiny, were tightened still further. This and the fact that he makes cheese only twice a week, not daily, persuaded Andreas to thermise his milk (see Glossary page 245) before cheese making.

He acknowledges, with a shrug, that there are raw milk purists (starting with cheese *affineur* Rolf Beeler) who lament this development but he's emphatic that using thermised milk has in no way compromised the character of the cheese. "And I'd rather that everyone who wants to taste my Schafnidelchäsli can do so without worrying." (Soft cheeses made from raw milk and ripened only a short time are not recommended for pregnant women, small children, the elderly, or

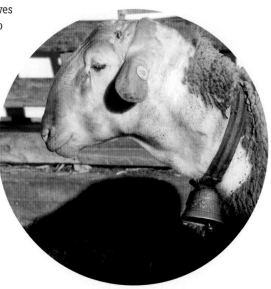

anyone whose immune system is compromised.)

Once thermisation is complete, Andreas cools the milk a little and adds the specific culture that will cause the rind to develop a soft white mould, and the rennet. Once the milk is set, he pulls a graceful, hand-held, butterfly-shaped cheese harp briefly through the curds to slice them. Then he exchanges the harp for a plastic shovel, drawing it backwards and forwards in the small stainless steel vat, gently lifting and cutting the curd into walnut-sized blobs. The lumpy mass is then piped over to a series of small, plastic moulds set on a stainless steel cheese table, which has draining holes to allow the whey to drain off.

The finished cheeses are later lowered into brine for 40 minutes, then stacked on wire trays and ripened in a cool, humid cellar. After about four days the white mould starts to bloom; within ten days, the plump little cushions are ready to be wrapped in film and affixed with Andreas's Schafnidelchäsli label featuring a rotund, curly-coated ewe and stamped with the Bio-Knospe bud, the Swiss seal of organic approval.

To appreciate this little sheep's milk cheese to the full, follow Andreas's advice, remove it from the fridge in good time and release it from its film to give it a bit of breathing space. Then prepare for a surprise. Cut into the soft, perfectly white, bloomy rind and you'll meet a delectably runny centre. The flesh is rich, smooth and creamy (sheep's milk has the highest fat content of the three cheese making milks), a bit like a perfectly ripened Camembert. The flavour – another surprise here – is agreeably mild (soft fresh sheep's milk cheeses do not have the assertive flavours of longer-aged, semi-hard or hard cheeses such as Pecorino or Manchego) with a nicely piercing point of acidity to give it a lift.

Today Andreas's range of products are made by the Hofkäserei Hofstetter in Entlebuch. Look out for Schafnidelchäsli in organic food shops throughout Switzerland.

Emscha GmbH
Glaubenbergstrasse
6162 Entlebuch LU

Tel. 041 481 01 01
info@emscha.ch
www.emscha.ch

Stanser Schafmutschli and Stanser Schafreblochon

Sepp Barmettler in Stans (see page 143) started making sheep's milk cheeses about 15 years ago. Two or three times a week he fetches the milk from several local farmers. Some of them keep floppy-eared, hornless Lacaune dairy sheep (of Roquefort fame) and others Ostfriesen, another noted milking ewe. If pressed, Sepp admits that he slightly favours Lacaune milk, which is even richer than Ostfriesen (sheep's milk has in any case a higher fat content than cow's). But he's content to have high-quality suppliers, whatever breed they keep, and happy with the results he's getting with their milk.

Sheep's milk is expensive – in Switzerland typically more than three times the price of cow's. For this reason, explains Sepp, "I experimented with cow's milk first – then, once I was satisfied with the result, I moved on to making the cheese with sheep's milk."

Sepp makes two kinds of Schafkäse. The first is Stanser Schafmutschli, a medium-sized, semi-hard, supple cheese that makes a fragrant addition to the cheese board. It also melts smoothly, which makes it a good candidate for raclette or for gratins. The second is Stanser Schafreblochon, a washed-rind, Reblochon-style cheese with a pinkish-beige crust and plump, creamy flesh that sags gently as it ripens.

The procedure is slightly different for the two sheep's milk cheeses. For the Schafmutschli, the milk is acidified first with imported French cultures and the

ing,
pelled
fmutschli.

Lacaune sheep.

rennet added, then it is left until firmly set. The curd is warmed to just about blood heat, cut into fairly small pieces ("like sweetcorn") and stirred until it reaches the desired texture and consistency. The prepared curds are tipped into moulds and pressed for about four hours to drive off surplus whey. Finally the Schafmutschlis are cellared for at least four and up to 12 weeks.

Stanser Schafreblochon.

For Stanser Schafreblochon, the milk is cultured, renneted and set, the curds are heated a little less than for the Schafmutschli, and water is added to dilute the curd and put a brake on acidity. Finally the mass is transferred to pierced, circular moulds with a diameter about the size of a CD, where it remains for 24 hours.

After a short spell in brine, the Schafreblochons are matured in Sepp's cellar for at least three weeks. Here they are subjected to the usual regular brushings with salt water to encourage formation of the rind and to develop the full, succulent flavour and gently yielding texture of the finished cheese. You can order both cheeses direct from Sepp online or find them at the Barmettler shop in Stans. Top delicatessens in Switzerland stock Sepp's sheep's milk cheeses, as well as a handful of superior cheese boutiques in the US. [See page 241.]

Sepp Barmettler
Barmettler Molkerei AG
Dorfplatz 9,
6370 Stans NW

Tel. 041 619 09 95
www.cheesenet.ch
jb@cheesenet.ch

Vivienne

Vivienne is a saucer-sized, washed-rind, sheep's milk cheese from Willi Schmid in Lichtensteig (see page 123). The milk for this dimpled little beauty – named after Willi's daughter – comes from a nearby farmer who keeps a small herd of Ostfriesen dairy sheep. Willi prefers them to Lacaunes (the Roquefort breed and the kind kept by Andreas Gauch, page 171), considering that Ostfriesen milk gives the kind of flavour and runny consistency that he's looking for in the mature cheese.

The milk is first acidified with the cheese maker's home-grown yogurt plus a couple of other cultures specific to this kind of washed-rind cheese. A dose of sheep's rennet is added – Willi prefers to match the rennet to the milk. When the curds have set to a smooth, thick mass, he heats them gently to lukewarm, cuts them in walnut-sized lumps and ladles them into small, perforated moulds. Once the curds are compacted by their own weight and the whey has drained off, the moulds are lifted away and the newborn cheeses are briefly brined. Then they're laid on shelves in the cellar to ripen for five to six weeks, with the customary turning and brushing with salt solution to encourage formation of the typical pinkish smeared rind. Finally the fragile little Viviennes

(weighing 300 g) are slipped into their round boxes and closed with a lid.

Willi ages all his own cheeses to perfection, rather than passing them to an *affineur* to do this for him. This way, when he releases them for sale they're good to go. But, he insists, there's still no rush for they'll keep a further couple of weeks with good refrigeration. Bring this delectable little cheese out of cold storage a couple of hours before you plan to dip into it, to allow the aromas and flavours to develop and to ensure that the cheese is properly runny. Serve it with good crusty bread, oatmeal biscuits, or pumpernickel.

Willi Schmid
Städtlichäsi Lichtensteig
Farbgasse 3
9620 Lichtensteig SG

Tel. 071 994 32 86
mail@willischmid.com
www.willischmid.com

- Bio-Schafskäse 8 Mt. alt
- Bio-Ziegencamambert
- Bio-Buffelmozzarella
- Schafsjogurt   u.v.m.

Bioschafmilchkäse
Terna

One of the best ways to sniff out small-scale, local cheeses is to track down a first-rate cheese shop in the neighbourhood and see what they recommend. It was during a behind-the-scenes visit to Hansjürg Wüthrich's Sennerei in Pontresina, an Aladdin's cave of local and international cheeses, that I first heard of Chatrina and Peter Mair, cheese makers in Tschlin. "*Sensationeller Schafkäse!*" ("sensational sheep's milk cheese") breathed Wüthrich, "you have to go and see them!"

Tschlin is a speck on the map in the lower Engadine, about as far as you can go in Switzerland before tipping over its southeastern edge into Austria. The village amounts to not much more than a cluster

of classic *sgraffito*-decorated houses, a beautiful medieval church, a small hotel, a village shop – and Chatrina and Peter Mair's cheese dairy.

The dairy's name is Che Chaschöl – meaning, roughly, "wow, what cheese!" in the local Romansh dialect, which you still hear widely spoken all along the valley. (Romansh, of which there are several local dialects, is one of Switzerland's four official languages, spoken by only about 30,000 people.) The Mairs took over the dairy and started work here in 2006. "To make artisan cheese, you've got to be a bit of an idealist!" acknowledges Peter, "you have to be convinced about what you're doing and you don't count the hours." For the Mairs, this means days that start at

The lovely architecture in the Engadine makes any trip to the region a treat for photographers (even if the weather wasn't ideal when we were there).

6 a.m. and seldom finish before 9 p.m. "We love what we do – our two boys are grown now, we have time!"

The Mairs make goat's, sheep's and cow's milk cheeses with milk from two organic smallholders in the village, both of them within walking distance of the dairy. The animals are milked twice daily, and the evening milk spends the night in perfectly refrigerated conditions: the churns are set in the ice-cold village fountain, refreshed throughout the night by a steady trickle of water fed by a mountain spring above the village.

Terna cheese from Che Chaschol.

Milk is cooled overnight in the village fountain.

The goats are hardy, stripey-faced Bündner Strahlenziegen and the cows silvery-grey Rhätisches Grauvieh – both of them rare breeds, indigenous to this steeply mountainous area and protected by Pro Specie Rara, the Swiss biodiversity foundation that protects rare plant and animal species and works to ensure their survival (www.prospecierara.ch). The Mairs set great store by sourcing their milk from local farmers who raise animals that are indigenous to this region. It's a real partnership with the *Bergbauern* (mountain farmers), a concrete way of supporting them as well as sustaining these rare breeds which would otherwise die out.

For the sheep's milk cheese called Terna (the Romansh word for 'basket', in which the cheeses are formed) the fountain-chilled evening milk is combined with the morning milk. The milk is pasteurised (see Glossary page 245) before cheese making begins. Seeing my raised eyebrow and doubtful expression (I admit to being a raw milk fan), Chatrina explained their decision to pasteurise the milk. "It's very simple: I'm not a trained cheese maker and I've had to learn every-

Peter and Chatrina Mai with some of their cheeses

thing from scratch, on the job, since we started four years ago. Raising sheep and goats is also something fairly new for our two suppliers." It seemed sensible to start out with the safety net of pasteurisation, she explains, adding that in due course the plan is to move over to raw milk.

Once pasteurised, the milk is cooled so that it's ready to receive the starter culture and the rennet. When the creamy milk has reached setting point, Chatrina cuts the curd with a hand-held cheese harp, then completes the cutting by dragging a plastic cheese shovel gently and rhythmically back and forth through the curds. Some of the whey is drawn off and replaced with an equivalent volume of water to slow down bacterial reproduction in the vat – cheese is a veritable bacteria incubator – and reduce acidity.

The curds are distributed between small plastic colander-like baskets set out on the stainless steel draining table. Chatrina cups her hands over the curds, pressing them down firmly into the baskets so that the finished cheeses will be attractively striated, like cheeses moulded the

old-fashioned way in rush baskets. Then she leaves them to drain for a few hours while she gets on with other cheeses – in a day, Chatrina makes three, sometimes four different kinds.

Later the Ternas will be brined for about ten hours before they embark on their eight-month ageing process in the cellar. At the start they will be brushed daily with a mixture of salt water and beer brewed in Tschlin's microbrewery (another artisanal business in this miniscule village). "It's not for the flavour of beer – you can't really taste it when the cheese is ripe," Chatrina reassures me, "it's to give the rind its beautiful, lightly tanned colour." After eight months the Ternas are ripe for eating, but they'll keep for a year or more.

We gathered around the kitchen table and nibbled on slices of Chatrina's one year-old cheese. It lived right up to Wüthrich's advance billing. The richness of the sheep's milk was balanced by just the right degree of acidity, the texture mildly crumbly and not too dense, the flavours lingering and complex. *Che chaschöl!*

Peter and Chatrina Mair
Cascheria Che Chaschöl
Giassa d'Immez 93A
7559 Tschlin GR
....
Tel. 081 866 35 01

MORE GOAT'S AND SHEEP'S MILK CHEESES

Caprinello
Willi Schmid
Städtlichäsi Lichtensteig
9620 Lichtensteig SG

Geissenfrischkäse
Susanne Klemenz
Galegge-Hof
4012 Suhr AG

Chèvre frais
Jean-François Burner
La-Croix-de-Luisant
1170 Aubonne VD

Geisse Bergkäse
Thomas Stadelmann
Käserei Stofel
9657 Unterwasser SG

Chèvre frais
Fabienne Andrey-Aebischer
La Chèvrette
1961 Vernamiège VS

Schafträumli
Franz Scheuber
Fläcke-Chäsi
6215 Beromünster LU

Chèvre frais
Michel Grossrieder
Fromagerie Moléson SA
1694 Orsonnens FR

Sufner Schafkäse
Dionis Zinsli
Sennerei
7434 Sufers GR

Formaggio di capra
Pietro Zanoli
Alpe Nimi
Valle Maggia TI

Tomme des Convers
Josef Spielhofer
Fromageries Spielhofer SA
2610 St-Imier BE

Formaggio fresco
formaggio stagionato
La Rösa
7742 La Rösa-Valposchiavo GR

Unterwasser Ziegenkäse
Thomas Stadelmann
Käserei Stofel
9657 Unterwasser SG

Frischer Geisskäse
Johanna & Walter Egger
3818 Grindelwald BE

BLUE CHEESES

Though legend has it that Charlemagne overindulged in blue cheese while visiting the monastery of St Gallen in eastern Switzerland in 778 (A.D.), it's unlikely that it was a home-grown blue – Switzerland has never had a tradition of such cheeses. Today, this is changing, however, and in various parts of the country, from Toggenburg in the east to Neuchâtel in the west, a few pioneering cheese makers are working with blue cheese.

The initial steps are the same for blue cheeses as for other cheeses: the milk is acidified with specific cultures and curdled by the addition of rennet, the curds are heated and cut and the cheeses formed. It's at the maturing stage that things take a different course. Blue cheese starts out life perfectly white. As the cheese ripens, the characteristic blue veins develop, giving it a marbled aspect and faintly mushroomy flavour.

•

Jersey Blue

As I made my way through the Toggenburg in eastern Switzerland one winter's morning, the freshly fallen, dimpled snow reminded me powerfully of lightly set curds in the cheese vat – that was when I realised the extent to which I'd got cheese on the brain. I was heading for Lichtensteig to find out about Jersey Blue made by famed cheese maker Willi Schmid (see page 122). It's a magnificent blue cheese similar in size and shape to a slightly lumpy Christmas pudding and enclosed in a thin, greyish, bloomy rind.

The milk for this unique cheese comes from a local herd of Jersey cows (hence its name) – something of a rarity in Switzerland, where bovine loyalties are about evenly divided between black-and-white and red-and-white breeds and Brown Swiss breeds. Jersey milk is famously rich, which helps to explain the cheese's lusciously creamy texture and flavour.

Willi makes Jersey Blue twice a week throughout the year, between 60 and 70 cheeses per batch. The rich, full-cream milk ("I like to work with whole, raw milk – none of it is skimmed") is warmed gently in a small stainless steel vat, then two starter cultures are added: yogurt from Willi's own production to acidify the milk, and a *Penicillium* mould sourced in Italy that causes the greenish-blue veins to form, and which gives the cheese a sweetly creamy flavour, closer to Gorgonzola than Roquefort.

Next comes the rennet to curdle the milk, which now rests quietly for about an hour till set to a smooth curd.

Willi unhooks his *Säbel* (literally 'sabre') from the wall and slices the curd in large pieces. Then he changes over to a pair of plastic pans, like deep dustpans, which he draws rhythmically back and forth through the vat to cut the curd in biggish lumps and release the primrose-

Jersey Blues before formation of the blue mould.

yellow whey that now floats to the top. He pipes the large lumps of soft curd over to a rectangular cheese table lined with cheesecloth, sprinkles on top a small batch of more finely cut curd ("for structure") and leaves it to drain while we go off for lunch.

In the afternoon, Willi works the drained curds gently by hand (he describes it as 'kneading'), a step which aerates them and lets in oxygen so as to allow the characteristic blue mould to develop. In the final step before ripening commences,

the (still white) cheeses are sprinkled with salt. Then they're transferred to the damp, cool cellar next door where blueing will proceed. It takes about eight weeks for the cheeses to ripen fully.

All Städtlichäsi cheeses are aged on the premises in Willi's temperature-controlled cellars – "that way I can keep an eye on them myself!" he says. You can buy them direct from the dairy in Lichtensteig, or at Globus and Manor or in specialist cheese shops in Switzerland, Germany and the US.

Willi Schmid plunges the sabre into the vat to cut the curd.

Large lumps of soft curd on the draining table.

Willi Schmid
Städtlichäsi Lichtensteig
Farbgasse 3
9620 Lichtensteig SG

Tel. 071 994 32 86
mail@willischmid.com
www.willischmid.com

Bleuchâtel

Bleuchâtel is a new blue cheese whose name elides *bleu* (blue) with Neuchâtel, the canton where it was born. It's made by Didier Germain at the *fromagerie* in Les Ponts-de-Martel, a small village in a chilly valley high up in the Jura. Bleuchâtel is Didier's baby: each year he produces only about 12 tonnes, compared with about 250 of Gruyère AOC, for which his *fromagerie* is also famous.

How come a noted Gruyère producer branched out into a semi-soft, uncooked, unpressed, blue cheese, a rarity in Switzerland? "*Par passion,*" responds Didier with a smile, explaining that he's crazy about Stilton and wanted to make a blue cheese for himself. "I went to England to find out how they make it." Back home in the dairy he began with tiny quantities – about 50 kilos of milk at a time, giving about 5 kilos of cheese. "We were really feeling our way – the neighbour's pigs got fat on my rejects!" It took eight months of fine tuning and intensive testing before Didier was satisfied with the result.

On arrival at the dairy the milk is immediately thermised (see Glossary page 245), a heat treatment that's a sort of halfway house between raw and pasteurised milk. Why not raw milk, as for many of Switzerland's great, traditional cheeses, I asked? Didier considers that heat-treating the milk in this way ensures a more even result. And the flavour? "You taste it, and let me know!" (He reminded me, in passing, that all Stilton is now made with pasteurised milk, heated to an even higher temperature than thermised – "and

it's a wonderful cheese!" I had to agree – and reserved judgment on his Bleuchâtel till I could taste it.)

After its mild heat treatment the milk is cooled and the special *Penicillium* culture is added (the same strain as for Roquefort) that will cause the blue mould to form as the cheese ripens. Once the rennet has set the milk to a thick, yogurt-like texture, the curds are briefly cut and stirred. The resulting large blobs are poured into holey plastic moulds and the whey left to drain out for the rest of the day, leaving white cylinders of infant

Note the piercings on the sides of the freshly pressed, brined, cheeses – piercing allows in oxygen which encourages development of the blue veins, below.

Bleuchâtel ready for sale.

cheese. These are brined for 24 hours, then moved to Didier's 'blueing room' and storage cellar above the village, where they rest on stainless steel shelves.

In order for cheese to develop the characteristic blue marbling, some blue cheeses are pierced with needles to open up the flesh and let in oxygen, which permits the starter bacteria to get busy. This is the system used by Didier. "At the beginning we stuck the cheeses with knitting needles," he grins. Looking for a more practical solution, he called on the local locksmith and together they devised a special cheese-piercing device: two heavy metal paddles with steel needles sticking out at right angles. The cheese is sandwiched between the paddles which are then cranked together so the needles penetrate the flesh and meet in the middle.

The needles are retracted and the pierced cheeses transferred to a cool, damp cellar next door. Here Didier turns them daily, scrutinising them to check that blueing is proceeding apace. After five weeks (and up to ten) the rindless cheeses are wrapped in royal blue foil stamped with the Bleuchâtel name. The cheese is sold in the dairy shop on the premises, in select cheese stores through-out Switzerland, in restaurants and at Migros in Neuchâtel.

With a few more visits ahead of me and no reliable refrigeration for cheese trophies till I got home, Didier offered to put some Bleuchâtel in the post. A few days later, a large box arrived. I opened it up, removed several layers of wrapping paper, extracted the cheese and peeled away the royal blue foil. Then I slid an extremely sharp, slender knife down the cheese to extract a sliver (cheese merchants use a wire to cut blue cheese, to avoid crushing the tender flesh). The pale ivory flesh was marbled with blue-grey streaks, the smell

Didier extracts a plug of cheese to check the development of the blue veins.

faintly – but appealingly – fungal. I tasted it carefully, thoughtfully – and quite privately. Damp and delicious, smoother and creamier than many Stiltons and less salty than Roquefort, it melted nicely on the tongue and left a satisfying, lingering flavour. Judgment was no longer reserved. I sent Didier an email with a resounding thumbs-up.

Didier Germain
Fromagerie les Martel
rue Major-Benoît 25
2316 Les Ponts-de-Martel NE

Tel. 032 937 16 66
info@fromagerie-les-martel.ch
www.fromagerie-les-martel.ch

MORE BLUE CHEESES

Berg Bleu
Christian Leuthold
Krummenbach 2
3775 Lenk im Simmental BE

Blaue Geiss
Willi Schmid
Städtlichäsi Lichtensteig
Farbgasse 3
9620 Lichtensteig SG

Blaues Wunder
Christoph Räz
Käserei Detligen
3036 Detligen BE

Bleu de Brébis
Regula Zwicky
Sur le Rang
2354 Goumois JU

Blue Star
Käserei Thalmann
Schaffhauserstrasse 4
8524 Uesslingen TG

→
The view down the valley
to Saanenmöser.

RECIPES AND SERVING SUGGESTIONS

You often hear it said that cheese should not be refrigerated. This probably dates from the time when people had cool, north-facing larders in which to store cheese, but few nowadays have such a facility. When you get your cheese home, remove any plastic wrapping, cover it loosely with waxed paper and put it in the vegetable drawer, which is more humid than the main part of the fridge.

When serving cheese, plan ahead: soft cheeses should come out of the fridge a few hours before a meal so they reach the correct, gently yielding consistency; hard and semi-hard varieties should remain refrigerated till an hour or so before eating, otherwise they begin to 'sweat'. The bloomy rind of soft cheeses is edible (and delicious), but most people prefer to cut away the rind from the stronger-tasting washed-rind and semi-hard varieties. The rinds of hard cheeses are seldom eaten. Some cheeses are naturally more pungent than others but cheese should always smell appetising and wholesome. Ammonia indicates the cheese is past its best and should be discarded.

All the cheeses featured in this book make worthy candidates for the cheese board. If you plan to offer a cheese course, keep the menu light so the cheese can really come into its own. A good lunch or supper formula is a main-course soup (fish and shellfish or a robust vegetable affair) followed by a selection of perfectly ripe cheeses and good bread.

While the finest cheeses – certainly the soft and semi-soft ones – are best served as a separate course, there are plenty that lend themselves to cooking. Here's a selection of recipes with cheese at their heart, some of them classics, others modern creations or adaptations.

Soupe de chalet

A classic soup from canton Fribourg, traditionally made in alpine chalets in summer, drawing on the simple ingredients available on the alp: potatoes and root vegetables brought up at the beginning of summer; wild spinach (and sometimes nettles) from the alpine pastures; milk, cream and Gruyère AOC from the dairy, and pasta from the store cupboard. The soup was traditionally served from a *dyètsè*, a barrel-like wooden tub typically used in canton Fribourg for cream. The tub comes with its own beautifully carved wooden spoon, with which guests are served.

Serves 6

– Put water and milk in a large pan and bring to a boil – make sure it's really large, otherwise it will boil over
– Peel the potatoes, carrot and onions and chop them roughly
– Add all vegetables to the boiling milk/water
– Season to taste with salt and pepper and simmer for about 30 minutes or until vegetables are tender when pierced with a knife
– Trim the spinach, chop roughly
– Add spinach to the pan with the elbow macaroni and cook for about 10 minutes or until the pasta is cooked
– Pull pan off heat, mix Gruyère AOC into the *crème fraîche*, stir it into the soup and serve at once in big rustic bowls

1 litre water

500ml milk

750g potatoes (about 6 medium)

1 carrot

2 medium onions

salt and pepper

a handful of spinach, about 100g (or 75g frozen spinach)

100g small elbow macaroni (*coquillettes*)

50g Gruyère AOC, grated

100ml *crème fraîche*

Wurstsalat – sausage and cheese salad

You can't get much more typical than Wurstsalat: smoked pork sausages divested of their casings, finely sliced, mixed with slices of mild cheese and given a crunchy garnish of chopped gherkins and shallots and a sharp mustard dressing.

Serves 4

Mixed salad leaves (lettuce, radicchio, rocket, spinach etc.)
– about 250g

4 Klöpfer/Cervelas sausages

100g mild cheese
(e.g. Emmentaler AOC, Tilsiter, Bündner Bergkäse)

a handful of gherkins, finely chopped

1 shallot or spring onion, cut in thin rings

a handful of cherry tomatoes, halved

2 hard-boiled eggs, shelled and quartered

chopped chives or lovage sprigs to garnish

– Arrange the salad leaves on a large platter
– Skin the sausages and slice thinly on the diagonal
– Slice cheese finely, then cut in thin strips
– Arrange the sausages and cheese over the salad, sprinkle with the chopped gherkins and shallot or spring onion and surround with halved tomatoes and quartered eggs
– Whisk together the ingredients for the dressing with a wire whisk or hand-held blender till thick and emulsified
– Drizzle dressing over the salad, sprinkle with snipped chives and/or finely chopped lovage

Dressing

---

1 tbsp mustard

salt and pepper

6 tbsp olive or vegetable oil

3 tbsp wine vinegar

1 tbsp mayonnaise

Autumn salad with pears, walnuts and Tête de Moine AOC

A beautiful, bitter-sweet-salty mixture of radicchio and lettuce leaves, sliced pears and rosettes of Tête de Moine AOC cheese.

Serves 8

━━━━━━━━━━━━━━━━━

A mixture of lettuce and radicchio leaves

2 perfectly ripe, unblemished pears – Red Williams if possible

Tête de Moine AOC rosettes

walnut halves

Dressing

━━━━━━━━━━━━━━━━━

1 tbsp mustard

salt and pepper

6 tbsp walnut or olive oil

2 tbsp lemon juice or wine vinegar

1 tsp honey

– Wash and spin dry the lettuce and radicchio in a salad spinner
– Arrange a selection of both leaves on six plates
– Wash the pears, quarter and core them and slice very thinly almost through, but leaving a 'hinge' on
– Splay out the pear quarters on top of the salad leaves (like a fan)
– Arrange Tête de Moine AOC rosettes around
– Roughly chop the walnuts and sprinkle on top
– Shake all the dressing ingredients together in a jam jar and spoon over the salads

Kohlrabi salad with shaved Sbrinz AOC and Bündnerfleisch

The earthy crunchiness of kohlrabi goes well with sharp Sbrinz AOC and pungent Bündnerfleisch (air-dried beef) in this savoury winter salad. Serve with crusty bread.

Serves 4

700g kohlrabi
(about 3, tennis ball-size)

salt

6-8 small radicchio leaves

50g thinly sliced Bündnerfleisch
(air-dried beef), cut in strips

a 50g chunk of Sbrinz AOC cheese

a handful of shelled walnuts

– Trim and peel the kohlrabi, discarding any hard, woody bits
– Cut them in half, slice thinly and cut the slices in thin strips
– Put in a colander, sprinkle with salt and leave in the sink for 2-3 hours to release some of their juice
– Shred the radicchio finely and cut the Bündnerfleisch in thin strips
– Take shavings of Sbrinz AOC off the cheese using a potato peeler or cheese parer
– Put the kohlrabi on a serving plate or in a bowl, mix with shredded radicchio and Bündnerfleisch
– Shake together all the ingredients for the dressing in a jam jar until emulsified and thick, pour it over the salad and toss all the ingredients together
– Scatter Sbrinz AOC and walnuts on top.

Dressing

2 tbsp white wine vinegar

1 tsp Dijon mustard

½ tsp salt

lots of freshly ground pepper

6 tbsp olive oil or sunflower oil

1 tbsp chopped parsley and chives

a pinch of sugar

Carpaccio of roast beetroot on lamb's lettuce with soft fresh goat's cheese and balsamic dressing

For this vibrant ruby red, white and green salad, the beets are roasted, peeled, thinly sliced and arranged on a bed of lamb's lettuce 'tongues'. If you can't find uncooked beetroot, use ready cooked and skip the roasting step. The salad is drizzled with a balsamic dressing and garnished with soft fresh goat's cheese. An alternative garnish of shaved Sbrinz also works well.

Serves 4-6

4-6 medium beetroot, uncooked

1 tbsp olive oil

coarse salt and coarsely ground black pepper

200g lamb's lettuce
(*Nüsslisalat/mâche*)

3 tbsp olive oil

1 tbsp balsamic vinegar

150g soft fresh goat's cheese, sliced or cubed

– Remove greenery from fresh beetroot, scrub them well but do not peel or trim
– Place them on a large sheet of foil, sprinkle with oil, salt and pepper
– Close up the foil to make a snug package
– Bake in a 180°C oven for 1½-2 hours or until the beets feel slightly soft when pressed, and the skin will rub off easily
– large ones will take longer than small ones
– Remove foil package from the oven and let beetroot cool in the foil
– When cool, rub off the skins or pull them away with a small sharp knife
– Slice the beetroot very thinly
[If using cooked, peeled beetroot, skip the preceding steps and just slice them very thinly]
– Pull the leaves off some of the lamb's lettuce and arrange them around the edge of the plates, like little green tongues
– Arrange the beetroot slices in concentric circles inside the ring of lamb's lettuce
– Mix together the olive oil and balsamic vinegar and drizzle over the beetroot slices
– Arrange some lamb's lettuce florets in the centre of the beets and scatter cubes of goat's cheese on top

Cheese terrine

A terrine with a difference – it's not cooked, but gets its name from the dish (terrine) in which several different types of cheese are layered, then refrigerated till firm, turned out and sliced. It's a neat way to present the cheese course – and excellent for using up odds and ends that are no longer quite presentable enough (or large enough) for the cheese board. Be sure to use a combination of soft and hard cheese, so the terrine holds together, and different colours so the layers look good when the terrine is sliced. Serve as a cheese course with walnuts and some dressed salad leaves, or after a bowl of soup for a chic little lunch or supper.

Serves 6-8

500–600g assorted soft, semi-hard, hard and blue cheeses (e.g. Fleurette, soft fresh goat's cheese, Gruyère AOC, Appenzeller, Tilsiter, Bleuchâtel etc.), rinds removed, cut in ½ cm slices

some halved walnuts to garnish

some lamb's lettuce or other seasonal salad leaves

chutney or *mostarda* to serve

– Brush out a small rectangular terrine or other deep, straight-sided dish (14 x 9 x 5cm deep) with oil
– Take a large piece of clingfilm and press it firmly into the corners of the terrine
– Arrange layers of sliced cheese in the terrine, going right to the edge with each layer – press the cheese flat as you go so there are no spaces, and keep a balance of textures and colours – start with hard, then successive layers of soft, semi-hard, blue, hard etc. Start and finish with hard cheese – this holds things together and makes the terrine easier to cut
– Close the clingfilm up over the top, cover with a lid or foil and refrigerate for several hours or overnight
– Remove terrine from the fridge an hour or two before needed, which makes it easier to unmould
– Open up the clingfilm, invert the terrine, turn it out onto a board and peel away the clingfilm
– Cut terrine in slices with a very sharp knife, bracing the slices with a spatula or your hand so they don't crumble as you cut them
– Lay slices on plates, garnish with walnuts and serve with dressed lamb's lettuce leaves and chutney or *mostarda*

Fondue

To many non-Swiss, fondue is a bit of a Seventies cliché; in Switzerland it's just an uncomplicated, convivial, warming winter dish, whose composition varies from region to region. You can get creative and come up with your own mixture if you like – aim for a mix of feisty/tasty hard cheeses (Gruyere AOC, L'Etivaz AOC, Berner Alpkäse, a little Sbrinz AOC), a mild one such as Emmentaler AOC and some semi-hard cheese to give the right unctuous consistency (Vacherin Fribourgeois AOC, Tilsiter, Appenzeller, Tête de Moine AOC etc.). A good rule of thumb is 150–200g rindless cheese per person.

– Cut the bread in good chunks, making sure that each chunk has some crust, otherwise the bread will fall apart in the fondue
– Put all the grated cheese in an earthenware fondue pan with the crushed garlic, wine, lemon juice and nutmeg
– Mix the cornflour into the Kirsch and stir until smooth, add to the pan, bring the cheese very gently to a simmer, stirring continuously (tradition dictates that fondue should be stirred in a figure of eight)
– Season with pepper
– Light the fondue burner and bring fondue to the table

Serves 6

plenty of good crusty French-style bread

900g – 1kg mixed hard and semi-hard cheeses, grated

1 clove garlic, mashed

400ml dry white wine

juice of 1 lemon

a little freshly grated nutmeg

2 tsp cornflour

1 small glass Kirsch – optional

black pepper

Ramequin

A classic Swiss dish, one of the many designed to use up stale bread and odd pieces of cheese. The chunks of bread are bathed in a mixture of eggs, milk and cream and grated cheese is sprinkled on the top. Perfect for brunch, or for supper served with salad and cold meats. If it suits you, pour the eggy mixture over the bread cubes in advance and refrigerate till you're ready to bake the ramequin.

– Lightly butter an ovenproof dish
– Cut the bread in chunky pieces, lay the pieces in the dish and sprinkle with white wine, if used
– Whisk together the eggs, milk, cream, salt, pepper and mustard in a bowl
– Pour it over the bread and leave for at least half an hour so the bread absorbs the liquid – or if you prefer, cover with clingfilm and refrigerate (up to 24 hours)
– When ready to bake the ramequin, heat the oven to 200°C
– Sprinkle cheese over the top of the dish
– Bake the ramequin for about 30 minutes or until golden brown and puffy

Serves 4

200g of stale (but not hard) crusty bread

optional: 4–5 tbsp dry white wine

3 eggs

300ml milk

200ml whipping cream

salt and pepper

1 tsp Dijon or coarse-grain mustard

150g semi-hard cheese (Vacherin Fribourgeois AOC, Bündner Bergkäse, Appenzeller etc.), grated

Sincronizadas (flour tortillas with ham and melted cheese)

When I returned to Switzerland after many years living in Mexico, I pined for *sincronizadas*, the ultimate Mexican fast-food snack – a pair of tortillas sandwiched with cheese (and sometimes ham), heated on a griddle or ungreased frying pan till the tortillas are piping hot and the cheese melted. Gradually tortillas began to appear in shops over here and I discovered that any Swiss semi-hard melting-type cheese (Raclette, Tilsiter, Appenzeller etc.) does the business perfectly. *Sincronizadas* were back on the menu. Serve with tomato salsa.

– For the salsa, mix together in a small bowl the chopped shallot, coriander leaves, green chili and tomatoes, add olive oil, seasonings and lime juice
– For the sincronizadas, heat a griddle or ungreased heavy frying pan over moderate heat
– Sandwich together 2 tortillas with cheese (and ham, if wished) and place on griddle/frying pan
– Press down with a spatula until you feel the cheese is beginning to melt – be careful the tortillas don't burn and reduce the heat if necessary
– Flip the sincronizada over and cook till the cheese is completely melted and beginning to ooze out at the sides
– Cut in quarters and serve with salsa

For each sincronizada you need:

2 flour tortillas or wraps

slices of semi-hard cheese (Raclette, Tilsiter, Appenzeller, Vacherin Fribourgeois AOC, Bündner Bergkäse etc.), rinds removed, enough to cover the surface of a tortilla

optional: a slice/slices of ham the size of the tortilla

Tomato salsa – 6 sincronizadas

1 shallot or spring onion

a handful of coriander leaves

1 fresh green chili, seeds removed, chopped

2–3 tomatoes

2 tbsp olive oil

salt and pepper

juice of 1 lime

Brik pastry parcels with prosciutto and cheese

Brik leaves, originally from north Africa, are like very thin crêpes – use filo pastry sheets if you can't find them. The brik leaves/filo sheets are filled with sliced cheese and prosciutto, folded up into parcels, brushed with olive oil and baked till golden and crisp. Serve over (or with) salad.

Makes 6 parcels:

200g hard or semi-hard cheese (Gruyère AOC, Appenzeller, Tilsiter, Raclette)

6 slices prosciutto or other cured ham (e.g. jambon cru, Rohschinken, etc.)

6 brik leaves (*feuilles de brik*)

olive oil to brush the parcels

– Cut the cheese in 6 rectangular slices, each about 30g and measuring roughly 10 x 5cm
– Wrap the cheese in the prosciutto
– Place prosciutto-wrapped cheese at one edge of each brik leaf or filo sheet, turn in the sides and roll it up to form a parcel, with the unsecured edge underneath
– Brush parcels with olive oil and place on a baking sheet lined with baking parchment
– Heat the oven to 220°C and bake the parcel(s) for about 10 minutes or until the pastry is golden and crispy

Cheese soufflé

While working on this book, I kept finding bits and pieces of cheese lurking in the fridge, looking for a home, so it was a delight to be reminded of this great classic. It doesn't much matter what cheese(s) you use, but it must be tasty and it must be Swiss! – Well-aged Gruyère AOC or Berner Alpkäse would be good, or a combination of semi-hard cheeses (Appenzeller, Tilsiter) with some Sbrinz for added punch.

Serves 4 as a starter
2 as a main supper dish

25g butter

3 level tbsp flour

250ml milk

salt and pepper

grated nutmeg

100g grated cheese

4 eggs

– Heat the oven to 200°C and butter a soufflé dish (18cm diameter)
Melt the butter in a saucepan, stir in the flour and cook for 2–3 minutes or until bubbly
– Add the milk, salt, pepper and grated nutmeg and stir vigorously until it boils and thickens
– Stir in the grated cheese and cook until just melted
– Draw the pan off the heat
– Crack the eggs one by one, drop the whites into a mixing bowl and the yolks into the pan
– Mix the yolks into the cheese sauce base. Add a pinch of salt to the whites and beat them with an electric mixer or wire whisk till stiff and snowy – they should just hold their shape
– With a wire whisk, fold a couple of tablespoonfuls of egg whites into the cheese sauce base to loosen it up a bit
– Then tip the loosened-up sauce into the whites, lifting, turning and shaking the mixture through the whisk so as to incorporate the whites without knocking out too much air
– Tip the mixture into the prepared soufflé dish and bake in the preheated oven for 20–25 minutes or until well risen and a beautiful burnished brown on top
– Serve at once

Cheese and onion tart with Appenzeller and Tilsiter

This is my take on Appenzeller *Käsfläde*, from eastern Switzerland. I've tinkered a bit with the original recipe, combining Appenzeller and Tilsiter and substituting Greek yogurt for cream, which lightens things up a bit. Using *fromage blanc* in place of Greek yogurt, works well too.

Serves 4-6

250g shortcrust (piecrust) pastry (or a 30cm disc of ready rolled shortcrust pastry)

25g butter

2 onions, thinly sliced

150g Appenzeller, grated

150g Tilsiter, grated

2 eggs

150ml Greek yogurt
or *fromage blanc*

250ml milk

Salt and pepper

– Roll out (or unroll) the pastry to fit a 26cm quiche tin and prick it in several places with a fork to stop it puffing up during baking
– Heat the oven to 190°C
– Melt the butter in a saucepan and cook sliced onions until soft and slightly golden
– Pull them off the heat and let them cool
– Mix together, in a bowl, the grated cheese, eggs, yogurt and milk, season with salt and pepper
– Spread the onions over the pastry and pour the cheese mixture on top
– Bake tart in the preheated oven for 40-45 minutes or until golden brown, risen and firm to the touch

Lasagne with artichokes and blue cheese

A good supper or lunch dish, quickly made with store cupboard/freezer staples. Look out for frozen artichoke hearts in specialist frozen food stores (e.g. Picard) – it's a labour of love to prepare your own and the ones in jars are too soggy. You can use fresh or dried pasta sheets; if dried, check the package to see if you need to blanch them first.

Serves 4-6

25g butter

1 tbsp flour

350ml milk

150ml crème fraîche (thick sour cream) or whipping cream

125g Swiss blue cheese (e.g. Bleuchâtel, Jersey Blue)

salt and pepper

500g frozen artichoke hearts

25g butter

250g lasagne sheets, fresh or dried

– For the sauce, melt the butter, stir in the flour and cook for a couple of minutes
– Add the milk and crème fraîche or cream and bring to a boil, stirring all the time until it boils
– Lower the heat and simmer for 5 minutes – sauce will be only lightly thickened
– Crumble in the cheese and season to taste
– Heat the oven to 200°C
– Slice the artichoke hearts and cook them in butter for 8–10 minutes or until tender; season with salt and pepper
– Butter an ovenproof dish
– If necessary, trim lasagne sheets to fit the dish
– Spread a little sauce in the dish and put a layer of pasta on top
– Build up layers of sauce and artichoke hearts (3 layers of filling sandwiched between 4 layers of pasta)
– Finish with pasta sheets and a layer of sauce
– If using fresh lasagne, bake for 15–20 minutes; if dried lasagne, it will need 25–30 minutes – the top should be golden brown and bubbly
– If you prefer, the dish can be microwaved (though unless you have a combined grill-microwave, the top won't brown). Allow 8–10 minutes depending on the strength of your microwave and the depth of the lasagne.

Cheese, ham and olive Bread

A simple, yeastless bread baked in a loaf tin, with ham, olives and grated cheese (Gruyère AOC or Emmentaler AOC work well). Delicious cut in slices and served with drinks, or with soup.

Serves 8

---

3 eggs

1 carton (125ml) natural yogurt

125ml (½ cup) olive
or sunflower oil

150g flour

1 packet (11g) baking powder

150g hard or semi-hard cheese,
rinds removed, grated

150g ham, diced small

30 stoned/pitted green olives,
finely chopped

salt and pepper

– Butter a loaf tin (or use a silicone loaf tin, no need to butter) and heat the oven to 180°C
– In a large mixing bowl, or the goblet of a food processor, beat together the eggs, yogurt and oil
– Shake the flour and baking powder through a sieve over a piece of grease-proof paper
– Tip the sieved flour/baking powder into the egg mixture, folding carefully to mix it in
– Stir in the grated cheese, chopped ham and olives
– Pour the batter into the loaf tin and bake for 45–60 minutes or until the top feels firm and a skewer stuck in the middle comes out clean – prolong the cooking if necessary to make sure it's not gooey in the middle
– Cool the loaf on a rack

Potimarron (or butternut squash), parsnip and potato wedges with sage and Raclette cheese

A gutsy autumn dish of veggie wedges with sage and melted cheese – serve as a main dish, or to accompany grilled or roasted meat or fish.

Serves 4 as a vegetarian main course, 6 as a side dish

━━━━━━━━━━━━━━━━

500g potimarron or butternut squash

500g parsnips or celeriac

500g waxy potatoes

2 tbsp vegetable oil

coarse salt and freshly ground black pepper

6–8 sage leaves

150g Raclette cheese, coarsely grated or finely cubed

– Discard seeds from potimarron/butternut, cut flesh (no need to peel) in wedges
– Peel the parsnips or celeriac and cut in similar-sized pieces
– Quarter the potatoes lengthwise (no need to peel)
– Line a large roasting pan with baking parchment, fill with vegetables, sprinkle with oil, salt and pepper and mix up well with your hands so the oil is evenly distributed
– Scatter the sage leaves around
– Bake at 200°C for 40–45 minutes or until vegetables are lightly golden and crispy at the edges
– Remove from oven, sprinkle with grated/cubed cheese and return veggies to the oven for another 10 minutes or until the cheese melts

Gratin of courgettes, spinach and mushrooms
with grated Sbrinz AOC or Gruyère AOC

Courgettes are coarsely grated and salted, tossed briefly in a pan with spring onions or shallots, spinach and mushrooms, mixed with eggs, cream and melted cheese and baked till golden and puffy. Delectable with grilled meat or fish, or as a stand-alone supper dish – and practical as you can do all the prep work ahead and refrigerate the dish ready for baking.

Serves 6 as a side dish, 4 as a main course supper dish

750g courgettes

salt, olive oil

1 onion, finely chopped

1 clove garlic, mashed

a handful of spinach leaves (about 150g), roughly chopped

250g mushrooms, finely chopped

3 eggs

200ml *crème fraîche*

pepper and nutmeg

50g grated Sbrinz AOC or Gruyère AOC

– Grate the courgettes coarsely using a cheese grater or food processor with grating blade fitted
– Put grated courgettes in a colander in the sink and sprinkle with one tablespoon salt. Leave to drain for about 30 minutes while you get on with the rest
– Heat the olive oil in a large frying pan and fry the onion and garlic till soft and lightly golden
– Add the spinach and mushrooms, cover the pan and cook for about 5 minutes or until the mushrooms release their juice and the spinach is wilted
– Uncover, raise the heat and cook hard, stirring, to evaporate any remaining juices
– Squeeze the salted courgettes to expel most of their moisture, add them to the pan and toss over high heat for 2–3 minutes, stirring
– Season with pepper, pull the pan off the heat and allow the vegetables to cool
– Put the eggs and cream in a bowl, season to taste with salt, pepper and nutmeg and mix with a wire whisk
– Mix in the cooled vegetables
– Lightly butter an ovenproof dish and tip the mixture into it
– If not baking straight away, cover the dish with foil or clingfilm and refrigerate
– Heat the oven to 180°C and bake gratin in the preheated oven for 30–35 minutes or until golden brown on top and slightly risen

Cauliflower and broccoli cheese
with walnut crumble

A two-tone cauliflower and broccoli cheese (use blue cheese, or any hard or semi-hard cheese) gets a gorgeous boost from a crunchy, nutty topping.

Serves 4

salt

1 bay leaf

500g mixed cauliflower and broccoli florets

50g butter

3 tbsp flour

500ml milk

150g blue cheese, crumbled, or hard or semi-hard Swiss cheese, grated

pepper

Crumble of:

50g walnuts

50g stale bread, cut in cubes

50g butter

a pinch of salt

– Boil a pan of water with a pinch of salt and a bay leaf
– Drop in the cauliflower and broccoli florets, cook for 5 minutes, counting from when the water returns to a boil
– Drain the cauliflower and broccoli and put them in an ovenproof dish
– For the sauce, melt the butter, stir in the flour and cook for a few minutes until bubbling
– Add milk, a pinch of salt and some black pepper and bring to a boil, stirring
– Cook for a few minutes until smooth and thick, then add the crumbled or grated cheese
– Cook briefly to melt the cheese, then coat the cauliflower and broccoli with the sauce
– Heat the oven to 200°C
– For the crumble, put the walnuts and stale bread cubes in the food processor or blender and process or blend till the texture of coarse breadcrumbs
– Add the diced butter and a pinch of salt (if butter is unsalted, otherwise omit) and process briefly to mix – the crumble should be quite chunky in texture
– Scatter the crumble over the cauliflower cheese and bake in the preheated oven for 20–25 minutes or until the sauce is bubbly and the crumble golden and crisp

Cheese pasties (turnovers) with bacon and potatoes

Outrageously calorific and utterly delicious, these are a sort of Swiss take on Cornish pasties: instead of meat and vegetables, the filling is of grated semi-hard, melting cheese (Raclette, Tilsiter, Appenzeller, Vacherin Fribourgeois), diced bacon and potatoes. Serve with a sharply dressed salad.

Makes 6 pasties

200g lardons (bacon bits), or streaky bacon diced small

400g firm, waxy potatoes (or new potatoes)

salt and pepper

200g semi-hard, melting Swiss cheese, coarsely grated

600g puff or shortcrust pastry

1 egg to glaze

– Put the lardons or bacon dice in a small heavy pan without extra fat and cook until the fat runs – don't let them get more than lightly golden
– Remove lardons with a slotted spoon and drain on paper towels
– Cook the potatoes in boiling salted water for about 15 minutes or until barely tender. Peel and dice them
– Cut the pastry into 6 equal-sized pieces, roll out each piece to a roughly circular shape
– Using a 20cm-diameter plate, trim each piece to a 20cm circle
– Put some cheese on one half of the pastry disc, add some bacon pieces and potatoes, top with more cheese
– Wet a border around half the circumference of the pastry, close up and press the edges together to give a pasty, or turnover
– Crimp the edges or press them together with a fork to give a decorative finish. Put pasties on a baking sheet lined with non-stick paper and brush with beaten egg
– Refrigerate until needed
– Heat the oven to 200°C and bake the pasties for about 20 minutes or until the pastry is golden brown

Polenta pie with leeks, cheese and walnuts

Choose a semi-hard (Raclette, Vacherin Fribourgeois, Appenzeller) or Swiss blue cheese for this rib-sticking supper dish, nice with cold ham or turkey, or as a stand-alone veggie dish. If you have access to the fat bolsters of ready-cooked polenta (like huge yellow sausages), use two of these instead of preparing your own polenta.

Serves 8-10

600ml milk + 600ml water
or stock

salt and pepper

250g medium-fine, quick-cook polenta flour (or 2 ready-cooked polenta rolls)

4 leeks, about 500g

15g + 50g butter

2 tbsp flour

600ml milk

1 bay leaf

150g semi-hard or blue cheese, grated or crumbled

4 tbsp chopped walnuts

flat-leaf parsley to garnish

– Make up the polenta with milk, water, salt, pepper and polenta flour, following instructions on the packet
– Tip cooked polenta onto an oiled sheet of foil, spread it out to a rectangle about 1cm thick and leave to cool till quite firm. (If using ready-cooked polenta, simply slice the rolls 1cm thick)
– Trim and wash the leeks, cut in thick-ish slices and put them in a shallow pan with 15g of butter, salt, pepper and half a cup of water
– Bring to a boil and cook steadily till the water has evaporated and the leeks are crunchy-tender (about 10 minutes)
– Heat 50g butter in a saucepan, stir in the flour and cook till bubbly
– Add the milk, bay leaf and salt and pepper to taste – bring to a boil, stirring, and simmer for about 10 minutes or until thick
– Fish out the bay leaf, add the cheese
– Butter a large, deep ovenproof dish and smear a thin layer of sauce in the bottom
– Cut the polenta in three pieces, put one piece in the dish (cut to fit if necessary), cover with half the leeks and some sauce
– Repeat with more polenta, remaining leeks and some sauce
– Finish with remaining polenta and a final layer of sauce. (If using ready-cooked polenta slices, layer them in the dish with the leeks and sauce as above.)
– Sprinkle walnuts on top
Refrigerate if not baking the dish at once
– Heat the oven to 200°C and bake the dish for 25–30 minutes or until golden brown and bubbly
– Sprinkle with chopped parsley to serve

Double-decker Rösti 'sandwich' with melted cheese

The original recipe for this wonderful crusty Rösti sandwich with melted cheese in the middle came from my neighbour. She uses Munster but you can use any semi-hard melting cheese such as Raclette, Vacherin Fribourgeois, Appenzeller etc. The recipe serves two for supper; for four, double up all the quantities. A lamb's lettuce salad makes a nice, sharp contrast.

Serves 2

500g firm, waxy potatoes (e.g. Nicola, Charlotte)

salt and pepper

2 tbsp vegetable or olive oil

slices of cheese to cover the surface of the Rösti, about 100g

- Peel the (raw) potatoes and grate them coarsely
- Put them in a bowl and season with salt and pepper (proceed immediately with the recipe, otherwise they will discolour)
- Heat a film of oil in a small, heavy frying pan (about 15cm bottom diameter)
- Tip in half the grated, seasoned potatoes to form a thick pancake
- Cover with a lid and cook over moderate heat for 7–8 minutes or until the underside is golden and crusty
- Invert the Rösti onto the lid, heat a little more oil in the pan, slide the Rösti back into the pan, replace the lid and cook the second side for 6–7 minutes
- Tip the Rösti onto a plate
- Heat more oil in the pan, tip in the remaining potatoes, cover and cook for 6–7 minutes as before
- Invert Rösti onto the lid, heat the remaining oil in the pan, slide the Rösti back into the pan
- Arrange the sliced cheese over the cooked side of the second Rösti, put the first Rösti on top, cover the whole thing with the lid and cook for a further 6–7 minutes or until the underside is golden brown and the cheese melted

Cheese Events and Markets

Concours suisse des produits du terroir:
Huge, tented market selling typical, local products from all over Switzerland including many fine cheeses, held in autumn every second year in Courtemelon near Delémont in the Jura
info@concours-terroir.ch / www.concours-terroir.ch

Salon Suisse des Goûts et Terroirs
Event/market held annually in autumn in the Espace Gruyère in Bulle to celebrate typical, local products, with a big cheese presence
salon@gouts-et-terroirs.ch / www.gouts-et-terroirs.ch

Chästeilet on Mägisalp
Annual mid-September event to celebrate the end of summer, with oompa-pa music, a procession of cows from the alp and partying into the night.
Tourist Information Hasliberg / 6084 Hasliberg Wasserwendi / Tel. 033 972 51 51 / www.haslital.ch

Chästeilet Justistal
Annual end-of-summer festival and distribution of cheeses in the Justistal, near Beatenberg
Gunten-Sigriwsil Tourismus / 3655 Sigriswil / Tel. 033 251 12 35

Alpine Cheese Festival on the Grosse Scheidegg, Grindelwald
Annual autumn event with alpine cheese, butter and bread sold directly from the granary, plus folk music and yodelling
Grindelwald Tourismus / Postfach 124, 3818 Grindelwald / Tel. 033 854 12 12 / www.grindelwald.com

Bagnes, Capitale de la Raclette
Annual, end-September event in Le Châble (near Verbier) featuring Raclette cheese from the Val de Bagnes
Verbier St-Bernard / 1934 Le Châble / Tel. 027 776 16 82 / www.verbier-st-bernard.ch

Muotataler Alpchäsmärcht
Annual alp cheese market held in autumn in the Muotathal
www.alpkaesemarkt.ch

La Désalpe, L'Etivaz
Annual end-September/early October celebration of the end of summer in and around the village of
L'Etivaz with processions of flower-decorated cows, goats and pigs and alphorns, singing and dancing
La Maison de l'Etivaz / Route des Mosses 72, 1660 L'Etivaz / Tel. 026 924 70 60 / www.etivaz-aoc.ch

Swiss Cheese Festival Huttwil
Annual end-September cheese festival in the Emmental
Pro Regio Huttwil / Marktgasse 1 / 4950 Huttwil / Tel. 062 962 55 05 / www.cheese-festival.ch

Museums

Musée gruérien
Rue de la Condémine 25 / 1630 Bulle / Tel. 026 916 10 10
info@musee-gruerien.ch / www.musee-gruerien.ch

Swiss Open-Air Museum Ballenberg
Century-old buildings, demonstrations of local crafts,
with cheese-making demonstrations in an historically authentic setting
Museumsstrasse 131 / 3858 Hofstetten / Tel. 033 952 10 30 / www.ballenberg.ch

La Maison du Gruyère
Place de la Gare 3 / 1663 Pringy / Tel. 026 921 84 00 / www.lamaisondugruyere.ch

Tête de Moine Cheese Museum of Bellelay
2713 Bellelay / Tel. 032 484 03 16 / info@domaine-bellelay.ch / www.domaine-bellelay.ch

Riederalp Alpine Museum
Riederalp Mörel Tourismus, Bahnhofstrasse 7, 3987 Riederalp, Tel. 027 928 60 50
www.alpmuseum.ch

Specialist Swiss cheese suppliers

Barmettler Molkerei AG
Dorfplatz 9, 6370 Stans, Tel. 041 619 09 95
jb@cheesenet.ch / www.cheesenet.ch

Rolf Beeler
Wiesengrundweg 2, 5524 Nesselnbach,
Tel: 056 622 03 13
cheese@rolfbeeler.ch / www.rolfbeeler.ch

Chäs & Co.
Grubenstrasse 38, 8045 Zurich,
Tel. 044 201 61 11
info@cheeseundco.ch / www.kaesereich.ch

Chäs Stadelmann
Geissmattstr. 7, 6004 Luzerne, Tel. 041 240 06 06
(also present at Luzerne market Tuesdays and
Saturdays)
info@stadelkaese.ch / www.stadelkaese.ch

Käse- und Molkerei-Spezialitäten GmbH
Alex Wirth, Colmarerstrasse 10, 4055 Basel,
Tel. 061 381 85 95
alex.wirth@bluewin.ch
www.basler-milchhandel.ch

Glausi's Käsespezialitäten
Spalenberg 12, 4051 Basel,
Tel. 061 261 80 08

La Laiterie de la Tour
rue de l'Ancien Comté 40,
1635 La Tour-de-Trême, Tel. 026 912 72 86

Fromages Cuennet
Rue de Vevey 15, 1630 Bulle, Tel. 026 912 71 87
cuennet.fromages@bluewin.ch

La Maison de l'Etivaz
route des Mosses 72, 1660 L'Etivaz,
Tel. 026 924 70 60
maison@etivaz-aoc.ch / www.etivaz-aoc.ch

Sennerei Pontresina
via Cruscheda 3, 7504 Pontresina,
Tel. 081 842 62 73
info@sennerei-pontresina.ch
www.sennerei-pontresina.ch

UK

KäseSwiss
104 Druid Street, London SE1 2 HQ
www.kaseswiss.co.uk
rachael@kaseswiss.co.uk

La Fromagerie
30 Highbury Park, London N5 2AA
highbury@lafromagerie.co.uk
www.lafromagerie.co.uk

and 2-6 Moxon Street
Marylebone, London W1U 4EW
moxon@lafromagerie.co.uk
www.lafromagerie.co.uk

Mortimer and Bennett
33 Turnham Green Terrace, London W4 1RG
info@mortimerandbennett.co.uk
www.mortimerandbennett.co.uk

Paxton & Whitfield
93 Jermyn Street, London SW1Y 6JE
www.paxtonandwhitfield.co.uk

Selfridges & Co.
400 Oxford Street, London W1A 1AB
www.selfridges.com

Whole Foods Market Kensington
The Barkers Building, 63-97 Kensington High
Street, London W8 5SE
www.wholefoodsmarket.com/stores/uk

USA

Culture, the US-published cheese magazine, has a comprehensive online list of cheese suppliers throughout the US: go to www.culturecheesemag.com and click on Find Cheese

Artisanal Premium Cheese
483 Tenth Avenue 2nd Floor,
New York, NY 10018
www.artisanalcheese.com

Bi-Rite Market
3639 18th Street, San Francisco, CA 94110
www.biritemarket.com

Caseus Fromagerie Bistro
93 Whitney Avenue, New Haven, CT 06510
www.caseusnewhaven.com

Cheese Plus
2001 Polk Street, San Francisco, CA 94109
www.cheeseplus.com

The Cheese Shop
Carmel Plaza, Ocean and Junipero,
Carmel, CA 93921
www.thecheeseshopcarmel.com

Cowgirl Creamery Cheese Shop
919 F Street Northwest, Washington, DC 20004
www.cowgirlcreamery.com

Cowgirl Creamery Cheese Shop
The Ferry Plaza, San Francisco, CA 94111
www.cowgirlcreamery.com

Darien Cheese & Fine Foods
25-10 Old Kings Hwy North, Darien, CT 06820
www.dariencheese.com

Farmstead Inc.
186 Wayland Avenue, Providence, RI 02906
www.farmsteadinc.com

Quality Cheese (Caroline Hostettler)
14420 Old Hickory Boulevard, Fort Myers,
FL 33912
www.qualitycheese.net

Formaggio Kitchen
244 Huron Avenue, Cambridge, MA 02138
www.formaggiokitchen.com

Marion Street Cheese Market
100 S. Marion Street, Oak Park, IL 60301
www.marionstreetcheesemarket.com

Metropolitan Market
100 Mercer Street, Seattle, WA 98107
metropolitan-market.com

Murrays Cheese Greenwich Village
254 Bleecker Street , New York, NY 10014

and Murrays Cheese Grand Central
43rd St. & Lexington, New York, NY 10017
www.murrayscheese.com

Oxbow Public Market
610 & 644 First Street, Napa, CA 94559
www.oxbowpublicmarket.com

Pastoral Artisan Cheese, Bread & Wine
53 East Lake Street, Chicago, IL 60601
www.pastoralartisan.com

The Pasta Shop
1786 Fourth Street, Berkeley, CA 94710
www.pastashop.net.com

A. Russo & Sons
560 Pleasant Street, Watertown, MA 02472
www.russos.com

Rubiner's Cheesemongers & Grocers
264 Main Street, Great Barrington, MA 01230
www.rubiners.com

Southend Formaggio
268 Shawmut Avenue, Boston, MA 02118
www.southendformaggio.com

Show Dairies in Switzerland

Appenzeller Show Dairy
Dorf 711, 9063 Stein, Tel. 071 368 50 70
www.schaukaeserei.ch

Bellelay Abbey Historic Cheese Dairy
Clos Eclairon 52,
2713 Bellelay, Tel. 032 484 03 16
www.domaine-bellelay.ch

Emmentaler Show Dairy
Schaukäsereistrasse 6, 3416 Affoltern im
Emmental, Tel. 034 435 16 11
www.showdairy.ch

Engelberg Monastery Show Dairy
Klosterhof, CH-6390 Engelberg,
Tel. 041 638 08 88
www.schaukaeserei-engelberg.ch

Flumserberg Alpine Cheese Dairy
Alp Tannenboden, 8898 Flumserberg,
Tel. 081 733 00 23
www.sennenstube.ch

Gotthard Show Dairy
6780 Airolo, Tel. 091 869 11 80
www.ticino.ch/caseificio

La Maison du Gruyère
1663 Pringy-Gruyères, Tel. 026 921 84 00
www.lamaisondugruyere.ch

Samnaun Alpine Dairy
7563 Samnaun Dorf, Tel. 081 868 51 58
www.samnaun.ch (see Art & Culture)

Schwyzerland Show Dairy
Milchstrasse, 6423 Seewen-Schwyz,
Tel. 041 819 82 82
www.milchstrasse.ch

BIBLIOGRAPHY

Dalby, Andrew, **Cheese**, A Global History, Reaktion Books Ltd., London, 2009

Hugger, Paul, **La fromagerie d'alpage dans le Jura vaudois**, G. Krebs S.A., Bâle, 1971

McCalman, Max, **Mastering Cheese**, Clarkson Potter, New York, 2009

McGee, Harold, **On Food and Cooking**, Scribner, New York, 2004

Ridgway, Judy, **The Cheese Companion**, Quintet Publishing, London, 2004

Ruffieux, Roland & Bodmer, Walter, **Histoire du Gruyère en Gruyère du XVIe au XXe siècle**, Éditions universitaires, Fribourg, 1972

WEBLIOGRAPHY

www.patrimoineculinaire.ch
online database of Switzerland's traditional food products, including all the principal cheeses

www.switzerland-cheese.ch
Switzerland Cheese Marketing website, in German, French and Italian,
with cheese profiles, events and recipes

www.fromagesdesuisse.com
French-language website of Switzerland Cheese Marketing, with cheese profiles, events and recipes

OFFICIAL WEBSITES OF PRINCIPAL SWISS CHEESES
www.appenzeller.ch
www.buendnerkaese.ch
www.casalp.ch (Berner Alpkäse and Berner Hobelkäse)
www.emmentaler.ch
www.etivaz-aoc.ch
www.gruyere.com
www.raclette-suisse.ch
www.sbrinz.ch
www.tetedemoine.ch
www.tilsiter.ch
www.vacherin-fribourgeois-aoc.ch
www.vacherin-montdor.ch

Glossary

affineur a specialist who matures cheese in optimal conditions to bring it to a perfect state of ripeness, ready for sale and consumption.

alp a summer pasture situated on the slopes above the valley and the tree line.

the Alps the whole, great, snow-capped European mountain range (Alp is related to the Latin *albus*, white) that stretches from Austria and Slovenia in the east through Italy, Switzerland, Lichtenstein, Germany and France in the west.

Alpkäse, fromage d'alpage, formaggio d'alpe Hard or semi-hard cheese made only in summer in small alpine dairies from the milk of cows (and/or goats) that spend the summer up on the alp, grazing the alpine meadows (see also Bergkäse).

Appellation d'Origine Contrôlée (AOC) system designed originally in France, now extended to other countries, to protect the name and ensure the survival of traditional, typical products. In order to qualify, cheeses must meet certain specifications as to the type and origin of milk, the area in which the cheese may be made, the method of production and its physical characteristics. The EU has recently put in place a parallel (and overlapping) system of Protected Designations of Origin (PDOs). Switzerland has a number of AOC/PDO cheeses, including L'Etivaz, Emmentaler, Le Gruyère and others.

Bergkäse, fromage de montagne, formaggio di montagna semi-hard cheese made in small to medium-sized village dairies in mountainous regions all year round. The milk for Bergkäse may come in summer from cows grazing on the alp, but because the cheese is not made in an alpine dairy, it must be labelled Bergkäse (not Alpkäse).

bloomy rind natural mould like a soft down which 'blooms' on the surface of some soft cheeses as they ripen.

brine a saturated salt and water solution in which cheeses are immersed after shaping and before maturing.

(cheese) harp a metal device resembling the musical instrument strung with a series of parallel wires, used for cutting and slicing the curd. Commonly inserted into an electrically powered motor set above the cheese vat, cheese harps can also be hand-held and drawn through the curds by the cheese maker.

cooked cheese (hard cheese) type of cheese where curds are heated to between 50°C and 59°C (well below pasteurisation, and a long way off boiling) and the cheeses pressed and brined to eliminate maximum moisture, giving them great ageing potential.

culture (see also starter bacteria) bacteria added to milk at the outset of cheese making which acidify the milk by converting milk sugars (lactose) into lactic acid; sometimes supplied by a specialist laboratory, sometimes made from whey reserved from a previous cheese batch.

curds solid mass of milk proteins (especially casein) that result when milk is curdled or coagulated by the addition of rennet.

Denominazione d'Origine Protetta (DOP) Italian translation of Appellation d'Origine Contrôlée (AOC).

hard cheese (aka hard, cooked cheese) type of cheese where curds are heated to between 50°C and 59°C (well below pasteurisation, and a long way off boiling) and the cheeses pressed and brined to eliminate maximum moisture, giving them great ageing potential.

Mutschli small, semi-hard cheese, usually made alongside larger alpine cheeses, designed for quick consumption, not for long ageing.

pasteurised (or pasteurized) milk heated to between 62°C and 66°C and held at that temperature for 30 minutes; or to between 71.5°C and 74°C and held at that temperature for 15–30 seconds (aka flash pasteurisation or High Temperature Short Time processing (HTST)). For cheese-making purposes, pasteurisation kills off all bacteria naturally present in milk, including those that contribute aromas and flavours.

propionic acid bacteria produce the holes in certain types of cheese (e.g. Emmentaler) during the ripening process.

prealps (préalpes, Voralpen) area between the central plateau (the Mittelland) and the high Alps, extending from the Appenzellerland in the east through central Switzerland to canton Vaud in the west. Terrain ranges from gently hilly to positively mountainous (though few peaks are higher than 2000 metres) with rich alpine pastures and fertile valleys, ideally suited to dairy farming – some of Switzerland's most famous cheeses (Appenzeller, Tilsiter, Berner Alpkäse, Gruyère AOC, and L'Etivaz AOC) come from the prealps.

thermised (thermized, thermalized) milk has been subjected to heat treatment, commonly in a range of between 57°C and 68°C, and held there for 15 seconds. Thermised milk is often described as a sort of halfway house between raw milk and pasteurised milk; thermisation as a form of 'soft' pasteurisation. For cheese-making purposes, some of the flavour-conferring bacteria that are present in raw milk (and eliminated by pasteurisation) are conserved in thermised milk – see Vacherin Mont d'Or AOC (page 129), Vacherin Fribourgeois AOC (page 85), Mont Vully (page 119), Schafnidelchäsli (page 171) etc.

raw milk has been neither thermised nor pasteurised. For cheese-making purposes, raw milk retains all the bacteria that contribute an array of aromas and flavours that are absent in pasteurised milk cheeses, and partially present in thermised milk cheeses.

rennet substance derived from the fourth stomach of a recently slaughtered calf, which contains an enzyme that coagulates milk. Vegetarian rennet is made from fungal or bacterial sources.

semi-hard cheese type of cheese where curds are heated only to around 42°C and the cheeses lightly pressed and salted. Moisture content is higher than in hard cheeses, and ageing potential correspondingly lower. It is the largest family of Swiss cheeses and includes Raclette, Vacherin Fribourgeois, Appenzeller, Tilsiter, Piora and many more.

smear-ripened cheese (aka washed-rind cheese) cheese that is ripened by regular smearing or washing of the rind with brine and/or an aromatic solution containing herbs, wine, beer etc.

starter (or starter bacteria) alternative name for culture.

vat large vessel, in Switzerland mainly made of copper, sometimes stainless steel, in which the process of cheese making begins.

washed-rind cheese (aka smear-ripened cheese) cheese that is ripened by regular washing or smearing of the rind with brine and/or an aromatic solution containing herbs, wine etc.

whey the liquid that results when milk is curdled or coagulated by the addition of rennet.

List of illustrations and credits

All photography in *Cheese – slices of Swiss culture* was made on site by photographer Nikos Kapelis.

p2 **Nicolas-Marie-Joseph Chapuy (1790-1858):**
Allières with the chalet dated 1650 at Col de Jaman, at full moon; coloured lithography by Jean Louis Tirpenne (*1801) and Victor Vincent Adam (1801-1866), No. 12 from "Les Chalets", Paris about 1840. (ROST 2546)[1]

p24 **Anton Reckziegel (1865-1936):**
'Suisse – Chemins de fer électriques de la Gruyère' (Swiss electric railway of Gruyère), with the Castle of Gruyère and the peaks of Dent de Broc and Dent du Chamois in the background; offset printing after a colour lithography by Hubacher & Co., Berne about 1910. (ROST 2548)[1]

p15 **Kurt Wirth (1917-1996):**
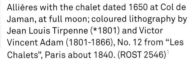
Cheese maker with harp at the 'Chessi' (cauldron); Gouache over a finely pencilled sketch on paper, undated. (ROST 1541)[1]

p28 **Sylvestre Pidoux (1800-1871):**
"POYA", *la montée à l'alpage* (Transhumance to the alp): Poyas are the stylised, naïf paintings formerly affixed to farmhouses depicting processions of people and cows as they make their way up to the high pastures for summer transhumance. Paper on fabric, under glass, tempera (egg wash), watercolour, about 1840.[3]

p18 **Emil Zbinden (1908-1991):**

Four original wood engravings 'Käse Verarbeitung' (cheese-making process) from a loose-leaf collection for the ZVSM (Zentralverband Schweiz. Milchproduzenten) 1973, wood engraving from the book by much-loved Swiss author Jeremias Gotthelf, *Die Käserei in der Vehfreude*, Büchergilde Gutenberg, Zurich 1944. (ROST 2585)[1]

p29 **Franz Niklaus König (1765-1832):**
'Fribourg. Berger des alpes de Gruyère'. (Fribourg. Herdsman of the Gruyère Alps); coloured lithography by Armand Emanuel Haller (1801-1834), about 1825. (ROST 1278)[1]

p29 Mathias Gabriel Lory fils (1784-1846):
'Marchands de Fromage. Canton de Fribourg'. (Cheesemongers of the Canton of Fribourg), the Alpine shepherd on the right is carrying the wheel of cheese on a so-called 'oiseau', a wooden frame for carrying objects on one's back, coloured aquatint on paper, 1822. (ROST 1379)[1]

p54 After Johann Heinrich Schilbach (1798-1851):
'Glacier Superieur du Grindelwald' (Upper Grindelwald Glacier) in the foreground the round-log mountain refuge hut with roof-covered viewpoint; blue-coloured aquatint at Johann Peter Lamy Publishers, about 1830. (ROST 2572)[1]

p38 Christian Schwizgebel (1914-1993):
Ascent to the alpine pasture, cheese-making kitchens on the upper left and right, dairy, storage and handling on the lower left and right, chalet at the centre; symmetrical 'Scherenschnitt' (paper cut), 1966. (ROST 1499)[1]

p59 MAP of the Sbrinz Route:
from www.sbrinzroute.ch with permission of Josef K. Scheuber.

p41 Edouard Girardet (1819-1880):
'Le Départ pour la Montagne' (Departure to the alp), a romantic farewell before departure to the alp above the Lake of Brienz; coloured aquatint etching by Gautier, published in Paris, London, La Haye 1862. (ROST 2577)[1]

p60 George Barnard (†1896):
'Passage of the Grimsel', the blasted out mountain trail above Inneren Urweid along the cliffs of the Grimsel mountain pass; Lithography from 'Switzerland – Scenes and Incidents of Travel in the Bernese Oberland – Drawn from Nature and on Stone by George Barnard', published by Thomas McLean, London 1843. (ROST 2576)[1]

p42 After an aquatint by Lory fils (1784-1846) and Franz Hegi (1774-1850):
'Heimkehr von der Alp' (Returning home from the alp), with Mount Wetterhorn in the background; xylography about 1860. (ROST 2578)[1]

p65 Schabziger:
Photographs of Schabziger are under copyright and provided by GESKA AG, Glarus.

p67 **Franz Grenier (1793-1867):**
Haslital (Bernese Oberland) woman carrying a wooden milking pail, holding the hands of her little daughter, with a dog in front of them; colour lithography on paper, undated. (ROST 2331)[1]

p80 **Emil Zbinden (1908-1991):**
'Jurahäuser im Sommer' (Jura houses in summer); four-colour woodcut, 1961. (ROST 2555)[1]

p72 **Johann Josef Geisser (1824-1894):**
depicting a cheese maker dressed in the traditional clothing of Eastern Switzerland working in a bar-turned vat, showing also a child, a dog and diverse cheese-making equipment. Watercolour, undated.[2]

p86 **Fondue:**
Marc Locatelli (*1954): Fondue illustration for the book *Ticking along with Swiss Kids*, published by Bergli Books, Basel 2007, watercolour, 2007.

p74 **Verena Broger-Bächer (*1943):**
Appenzeller ascent in snow to the alpine pasture with two alpine shepherds, six cows, four goats and one dog with the Alpstein chain of mountains in the background; colour lithography, 1980. (ROST 2547)[1]

p91 **William Henry Bartlett (1809-1854):**
'Airolo' at the south ramp of the Gotthard Pass, with the Tremola hairpin curves in the background; steel engraving by Thomas Jeavous (1816-1867), from *Switzerland* by William Beattie, published by George Virtue, London 1835. (ROST 2549)[1]

p76 **Josef Reinhart (1749-1829):**
'Costumes du Canton d'Appenzell Rhode intérieur' (Costumes of the Canton of Appenzell Innerrhoden); colour print after the coloured aquatint at Birmann & Huber, Basel. (ROST 1940)[1]

p100 **Elisabeth Lentzen (*1933):**
'Käserei Steingrube' (Steingrube Cheese Dairy) in Oberburg near Burgdorf; watercolour, 1983. (ROST 2556)[1]

p110 **Jean-Louis Bleuler (1792-1850):** 'Vue du Glacier du Rheinwald prise près les cabanes des bergers de Bergame'. (View of the Rheinwald Glacier, taken from near the cabins of Bergamo shepherds): the highest Swiss alp on the route of the San Bernardino sumpters and at the place where the Splügen sumpters' route branches off; coloured aquatint, undated. (ROST 2557)[1]

p156 **Johann Jakob Biedermann (1763-1830):** Two young herdsmen with four goats; etching on paper, undated. (ROST 2456)[1]

p112 **Edmond Bille (1878-1959):** 'Raclette in the alpine dairy'; five-colour lithography on paper, 1927. (ROST 2009)[1]

210

Photograph courtesy of Switzerland Cheese Marketing.

p146 **William Collingwood Smith (1815-1887):** 'The Bay of Uri, Lake of Lucerne' Boat landing at Brunnen with a covered rowing boat and view over the Lake of Lucerne of the snow-covered Mount Bristen; watercolour on paper, about 1840. (ROST 2575)[1]

238 **Sylvestre Pidoux (1800-1871):** 'POYA', *la montée à l'alpage* (Transhumance to the alp): Poyas are the stylised, naïf paintings formerly affixed to farmhouses depicting processions of people and cows as they make their way up to the high pastures for summer transhumance. Paper on fabric, under glass, tempera (egg wash), watercolour, about 1840.[3]

p152 **Nikolaus Weiss after Ludwig Vogel (1788-1879):** Das 'Gebet' (Saying grace). Figures are wearing costumes of the Canton of Berne, a wheel of Sbrinz is on the table; lithography on paper, undated. (ROST 2581)[1]

Inside back cover

A page 'Wie in der Schweiz der Käse entsteht' (How cheese is made in Switzerland), published by the Swiss Cheese Union, black print on beige paper, Berne, undated. (ROST 2884)[1]

Index

Edelweiss fabric | ˈeɪ.dəl.vaɪs | The | bot. [Leontopodium alpinum] | Edelweiß {n}
The exact origins of the fabric for the famous Swiss Edelweiss shirt, as seen on the cover of this book, are something of a mystery. This cotton Jacquard fabric, which is both extremely hard-wearing and soft to the touch, seems to have been made since at least the early 1960s in small mills throughout canton Bern. Originally the shirts were made by Heimatarbeiterinnen (home dressmakers). Gradually small firms such as Eisenstein Frères Biel (EFBE), Habis in Flawil, Lauterburg in Bärau, and Gugelmann in Roggwil, took over fabrication. Today, one of the biggest suppliers of both the fabric and a range of Edelweiss wear is EFBESA in Brügg near Biel. The shirts are still proudly worn by working farmers, wrestlers (Schwinger) and country music players. In recent times they have featured prominently on countrywide posters in a promotional campaign by the Swiss farming lobby, worn by 'real' farmers as well as by local and international celebrities. Nowadays, the Edelweiss fabric and shirt has achieved cross-over status as an item of Swiss country-chic, popular with locals as well as tourists.

Acknowledgements

Countless people helped to make this book happen, no-one more so than *Dianne Dicks,* publisher at Bergli Books, whose generous support and constructive editing have been invaluable throughout. I couldn't have wished for a better cheese companion than photographer, *Nikos Kapelis*, who travelled all over Switzerland with me, chatting up cheese makers and farmers in any of the country's chief languages, putting people at their ease and making the intrusive business of cameras, tripods and lights as painless as possible.

Special thanks go to all the artisan cheese makers who welcomed us to their dairies, patiently fielding our questions, offering hospitality (and great breakfasts) and plying us with samples: *Christoph Glauser* in Oberhünigen (Emmentaler); *Benoît Kolly* in Le Mouret (Gruyère); *Jean-Louis Roch* in Le Châtelard (Gruyère d'alpage); *Claude-Alain and Isabelle Mottier* in L'Etivaz (L'Etivaz); *Ernst and Margrit Kübli* in Saanenmöser (Berner Alpkäse and Hobelkäse); *Andreas Gut* in Wiesenberg (Alp Sbrinz); *Sepp Gut* in Buochs (Sbrinz); *Marcel and Lina Tobler* in Schachen (Appenzeller); *Reto Maag* and family in Rufi (Tilsiter); *Stephan Forrer* in Ftan (Bündner Bergkäse); *Alexander Zenhaüsern* in Obergesteln (Raclette and Gomser); *the Spielhofer family* in St Imier (Tête de Moine); *Louis Bérard* in Chavannes-les-Forts (Vacherin Fribourgeois); *Paolo Alberti* (cheese maker) and *Adriano Dolfini* (secretary of the Corporazione di Boggesi) up at Alpe Piora (Piora); *Ewald Schafer* in Cressier (Mont Vully); *Willi Schmid* in Lichtensteig (countless cheeses of his own creation); *the Hauser family* in Le Lieu (Vacherin Mont d'Or); *Sepp Barmettler* in Stans (various cheeses of his own creation); *Michel Beroud* in Rougemont (Fleurette and other own creations); *Serge and Claude-Lise Lenoir* in Glion (goat's cheeses); *François Jaquet* in Grandvillard (Le Vieux Chevrier); *Andreas Gauch* in Niederwil (Schafnidelchäsli); *Peter and Chatrina Mair* in Tschlin (various sheep's milk cheeses); *Didier Germain* in Les Ponts-de-Martel (Bleuchâtel).

I am grateful to *Manuela Sonderegger* at Switzerland Cheese Marketing for her unwavering support for the book, and to *SCM* for their contribution towards making it happen.

Thanks go also to the organisers of the Olympiades des Fromages de Montagne 2009 and the Swiss Cheese Awards 2010 for inviting me to serve as a cheese judge at both these events. *René Kolly*, President of Fromarte, and *Rolf Beeler*, cheese *affineur*, both gave me valuable insights into artisan cheese making in Switzerland. Special thanks also to *Ernst Roth* of the Roth Stiftung in Burgdorf, who read critically through the text and offered constructive suggestions that have certainly improved the finished text; and to his amanuensis *Julia Hausammann* who spent many hours sifting through images and artefacts for their potential suitability as illustrations for the book.

And finally, a tribute to my chief recipe tester, chauffeur to the farthest-flung corners of Switzerland and untiring – but not uncritical – supporter, *Monty Style*.

Sue Style, Bettlach, August 2011

About the author:
Sue Style (www.suestyle.com) is a British food, wine and travel writer
who has lived in Spain, France, Mexico and Switzerland. She is
now based in Alsace, close to Basel. Her articles are published in
Financial Times Weekend, Decanter, France magazine and other
UK-based publications and her many books include A Taste of Alsace,
Fruits of the Forest, A Taste of Switzerland and Honey, from Hive to
Honeypot. Cheese is a particular passion of hers and for this – her
ninth – book, she travelled the length and breadth of Switzerland to
meet the makers of the country's finest farmhouse cheeses, as well
as serving on the jury of the Mountain Cheese Olympics and the Swiss
Cheese Awards.

About the photographer:
Nikos Kapelis (www.nikoskapelis.com) was born in Greece and now lives
with his family near Winterthur, Switzerland. He studied photography
in Milan and Zurich. His work has been published in Marie Claire,
Financial Times Weekend and Zester Daily and in numerous professional
publications. This is his first major book. His special love is people –
meeting them, putting them at their ease, and photographing them at
work and at play.

About the Roth-Stiftung Burgdorf:
This foundation is located in the Kornhaus in Burgdorf and has a
collection of several thousand works of art, documents and books
regarding the history of Burgdorf and the Emmental valley as well as
objects relating to the culture and history of Switzerland's milk,
alpine and cheese industries. The foundation provides information for
research projects on request and can be visited by appointment only.
Email: rothstiftung@alporama.ch

About Bergli Books:
Since 1990 Bergli Books (www.bergli.ch) has published books in English
that focus on Switzerland, its people, culture and diversity.

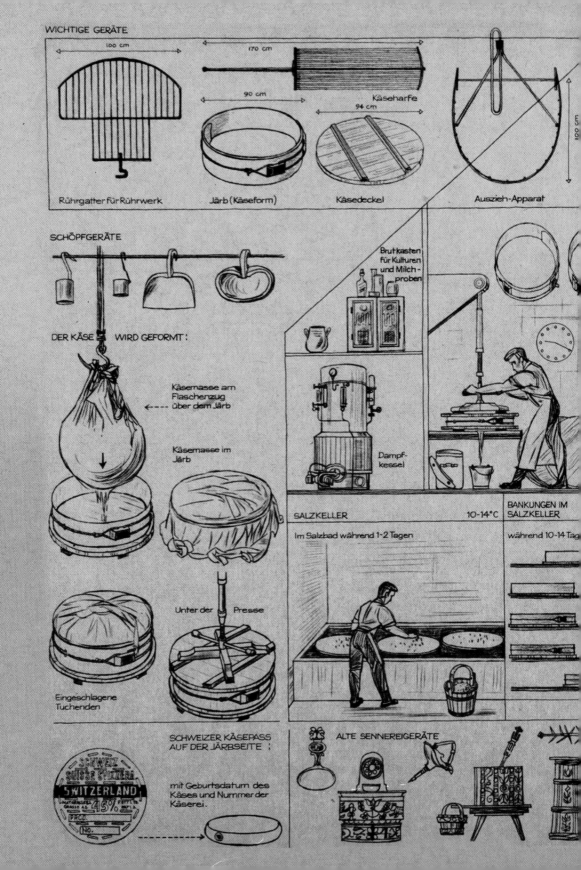

WICHTIGE GERÄTE

100 cm

170 cm

Käseharfe

90 cm

94 cm

190 cm

Rührgatter für Rührwerk

Järb (Käseform)

Käsedeckel

Auszieh-Apparat

SCHÖPFGERÄTE

Brutkasten für Kulturen und Milch-proben

DER KÄSE WIRD GEFORMT:

Käsemasse am Flaschenzug über dem Järb

Käsemasse im Järb

Dampf-kessel

Unter der Presse

Eingeschlagene Tuchenden

SALZKELLER   10-14°C

BANKUNGEN IM SALZKELLER

Im Salzbad während 1-2 Tagen

während 10-14 Tagen

SCHWEIZER KÄSEPASS AUF DER JÄRBSEITE:

ALTE SENNEREIGERÄTE

SCHWEIZ
SWITZERLAND
45%

mit Geburtsdatum des Käses und Nummer der Käserei.